'Modest and civil people'

Maynooth Studies in Local History

SERIES EDITOR Michael Potterton

This is one of six volumes in the Maynooth Studies in Local History series for 2022. It is also my first year as series editor, having taken over the role from the irreplaceable Raymond Gillespie, who held that position from 1995 to 2021, overseeing the publication of a veritable treasure trove of studies in those 27 years. Raymond established the series with Irish Academic Press as a direct result of the enormous success of the Maynooth MA in Local History programme, which began in 1992. Under Raymond's supervision, some 153 volumes were produced, authored by 140 different scholars (94 men and 46 women). The first volume, on education in nineteenth-century Meath, was written by Paul Connell, and the 153rd, on the Dublin Cattle Market in the 1950s and 1960s, was by Declan O'Brien. Eleven people have each contributed two volumes to the series, while Terry Dooley is the only person to have written three.

The remarkable collection now covers some 1,500 years of history across 31 counties, dealing variously with aspects of agriculture and fishing, architecture, crime and punishment, death and burial, economy and trade, education, famine, gender, healthcare, industry, language and literature, migration, music and the arts, politics, religion, society, travel and communication, urban development, war and much more besides. I am grateful to Raymond for entrusting the series to me, and to Four Courts Press for not vetoing the appointment. Together, I am sure that we can build on the sound foundations established over more than quarter of a century of diligent work.

The current crop of titles takes us from a broad look at religion and society in medieval Galway to a very specific and tragic event in Knockcroghery village on the night of 20 June 1921. En route we witness the gradual dismantling of Irish lordship in early modern north Co. Cork, and the development of nursing and midwifery in Co. Tipperary at the turn of the twentieth century. Finally, we have biographical sketches of two remarkable men of the nineteenth century – Thomas Conolly (1823–76) of Castletown House in Co. Kildare and botanist Nathaniel Colgan (1851–1919) of Dublin.

While the genesis and home of this series lie firmly at Maynooth, it is a mark of its appeal, its breadth and its inclusivity that this year's contributors are drawn from Carlow College, Glenstal Abbey, NUI Galway, Trinity College Dublin and the University of Limerick as well as Maynooth University.

Maynooth Studies in Local History: Number 158

'Modest and civil people': religion and society in medieval Galway

Rachel Moss & Colmán Ó Clabaigh OSB

FOUR COURTS PRESS

Set in 11.5pt on 13.5pt Bembo by
Carrigboy Typesetting Services for
FOUR COURTS PRESS LTD
7 Malpas Street, Dublin 8, Ireland
www.fourcourtspress.ie
and in North America for
FOUR COURTS PRESS
c/o IPG, 814 N Franklin Street, Chicago, IL 60610

© Rachel Moss & Colmán Ó Clabaigh OSB, 2022

ISBN 978–1–80151–028–8

Printed in Ireland
by SprintPrint, Dublin

Contents

For Brendan Kelly

Acknowledgments

We are grateful to Archdeacon Gary Hastings for his insights on St Nicholas', to Dr Michael Potterton, series editor, for cajoling us into doing this, and to Margaret Quinlan of Margaret Quinlan Architects for permission to use material from 'St Nicholas' Collegiate Church Conservation Plan' (Galway, 2021).

Introduction

Sometime during the year 1508, Stephen Lynch FitzDominick, a Galway merchant and four-times mayor of the town, returned home from a voyage. Noticing some building work on the hill overlooking the harbour, he enquired as to its nature and was informed that a new Augustinian priory was being constructed. Intrigued that such a major project should be undertaken without his knowledge, he asked about its patron and learned that it was his own wife, Margaret Athy, a devout benefactor of good causes, a Compostela pilgrim and, like Lynch, a member of one of the town's 'tribes', the fourteen merchant families who dominated its civic, economic and religious life. What his initial response was is not recorded, but Lynch went on to become one of the chief benefactors of the house, generously endowing the Augustinian community on his death in 1536.

Whether apocryphal or not, this vignette illustrates the remarkable flowering that occurred in the civic, economic and religious life of Galway in the late fifteenth and early sixteenth centuries. The extent of the settlement's transformation by its merchant rulers, particularly the Lynches, is evident in the idealized mid-seventeenth-century pictorial map of the town. Produced somewhere in the Spanish Netherlands and based on the recollections of the Galway priest Henry Joyce, its depiction of the town's residences, religious houses and civic buildings is largely confirmed by the surviving medieval fabric, most notably Lynch's Castle, the Spanish Arch and the Collegiate Church of St Nicholas.[1] The survival of the corporation archives makes it possible to trace developments in civic and social life from the establishment of the Galway mayoralty in 1484.[2] Likewise, the existence of an extensive dossier of ecclesiastical material illustrates the religious life of the town, particularly the way in which its unique ecclesiastical structure, the wardenship, operated.[3]

This study traces the interaction of religion and society in Galway from the establishment of a settlement at 'Bungalvy' at a crossing point of the Corrib or Galway river by Richard de Burgh in 1232.

It examines the evidence for the emergence of parochial structures and a parish church in the thirteenth and fourteenth centuries to serve the needs of the Anglo-Norman community. The townspeople's continuing self-identification as an English enclave proved an enduring point of conflict with their Gaelic ecclesiastical superiors – first the bishops of Annaghdown and then the archbishops of Tuam. This abiding sense of autonomy found expression in 1484 with the establishment of the wardenship of Galway. This unique arrangement meant that the town's ecclesiastical affairs were presided over by a warden assisted by a college of eight priest-vicars who operated almost entirely independently of episcopal oversight. This college of clerics provided a high level of liturgical and pastoral service to the community under the close supervision of the mayor and corporation. From 1296, with the establishment of a Franciscan foundation, the townspeople were exposed to the ministry and influence of the mendicant friars. This expanded significantly in the late fifteenth century with the establishment of friaries for the Dominicans and Augustinians, along with a house of Franciscan nuns.

Quite apart from illustrating the religiosity of the townsfolk, the establishment of these institutions and the extensive refurbishment and expansion of the Collegiate Church of St Nicholas is indicative of the town's prosperity. Evidence for personal devotion occurs in the surviving iconography of the saints, in the practice of pilgrimage and in the customs marking the high points of the ritual year. The church's rituals solemnized the key moments of transition like birth, marriage and death and occasionally spilled out onto the streets in corporate celebrations like the *Corpus Christi*, Rogationtide and Palm Sunday processions. In the moral sphere both the corporation and ecclesiastical records provide candid evidence of attempts to control the behaviour of the town's citizens and clergy.

Like many communities in late medieval Europe, Galway was a town in which 'Christ and Caesar went hand in glove' and where economic, religious and civic concerns were so intertwined as to be inseparable. With its quasi-independent civic and ecclesiastical structures, prosperous economy and extensive trading links, its aspirations lay poised somewhere between the ethos of the marketplace and the values of the 'City of God'.

1. Establishing the church

The earliest recorded place-name for Galway, *Bún Gaillimh*, reflects its strategic position at the mouth of a short river, the Galleamh, now known as the Corrib. This links the lake systems of loughs Corrib, Mask and Carra, navigable for about 145km northwards, into Galway Bay, an important natural deep-water port and shelter from the wilds of the Atlantic. The town itself is built across two ridges. The northern ridge, the longer of the two, supported *an Bóthar Mór*, the main road into the settlement from the east, while the second ridge terminates at Forthill.[1] Little is known of the early settlement of the area. The Uí Conchobhair (O'Connors) erected a *dún* or fort at this strategic location in 1124, the first definite evidence of a settlement here.[2]

The earliest Anglo-Norman settlement at 'Bungalvy', and its establishment as caput for the manor of Galvy in 1232 was initially met with strong resistance. The first de Burgh castle was destroyed after just a year, and its replacement met a similar fate in 1247. In this year the annals record the destruction of both castle and town, suggesting the formation of a settlement by this time. The destruction of the 'town' is again mentioned in *c*.1266, when the de Burghs were once more attacked by their Gaelic foes.[3]

Excavations in 2017 uncovered traces of both the Uí Conchobhair *dún* and the 1232 de Burgh castle, indicating that the Anglo Normans had utilized the site of the earlier fortification.[4] This was located on the eastern side of the river. The choice of site was doubtless to maintain control over the important north–south routeway up the River Corrib to the lakes beyond, and over eastern access to the natural harbour at Galway.

EARLY ECCLESIASTICAL HISTORY

If the origins of the settlement at Galway are obscure, its early ecclesiastical history is even more opaque.[5] Despite its strategic position, there is no clear evidence of an early Irish monastic settlement at the site and the nearest significant ecclesiastical centre was at Roscam, farther east along the bay. It is possible, as argued below, that an early chapel occupied the site of the current church of St Nicholas, while the chapel of St Mary-on-the-Hill on the northern bank of the Corrib is attested by the early thirteenth century.

Galway and its surrounding territory formed part of the diocese of Annaghdown before the Synod of Kells in 1152. The rectory of 'Lismacuan' [the fort of the harbour] in the territory of 'Clonferg', located to the east of Lough Corrib, and extending as far south as Galway itself, was granted to the Cistercian community of Abbeyknockmoy sometime between its foundation *c*.1190 and 1201.[6] James Hardiman conjectured that this was the early settlement at Galway. If this was the case, it seems likely that an early chapel was established or annexed by the Cistercians.[7] That an early church was present in Galway is supported by the 1303–6 ecclesiastical taxation, which notes that the church of Galway, and the neighbouring parish of Oranmore, were possessions of the Cistercians at Abbeyknockmoy at that time.[8] This was an Uí Conchobhair foundation and one of the few Cistercian monasteries established west of the Shannon. It was situated in the diocese of Tuam, whose archbishops generally supported the monks in any disputes that arose with their parishioners in Galway. This connection also benefitted successive archbishops in their ongoing attempts to have the see of Annaghdown amalgamated with Tuam.

EARLY CHAPELS IN GALWAY

The medieval church of St Nicholas is located on the prominent tip of one of two ridges that juts towards Galway Bay, near where the ancient *Bóthar Mór* comes to its terminus. The presence of an early Christian church along a major routeway and adjacent to the Gaelic *dún* would not be unexpected, but no evidence of this has yet revealed itself; the curved street plan to the west of the current church more likely the result of natural topography than the ghost of an earlier circular enclosure.

Accounts of the history of the parish church have suggested variously the presence of 'a small chapel soon before in this place';[9]

a chapel of the Knights Templar, 'the original and only place of worship belonging to the settlers';[10] and a chapel that was either a Templar church, or a chapel dedicated to St Nicholas.[11]

The suggestion that the church occupied the site of a Knights Templar chapel is without foundation; there is no contemporary historical mention of that order in Galway before their disbandment.[12] As a crusading order, their presence in a port town might be expected, although more typically preceptories were located in rural areas, close to the agricultural estates that supported them. Templar chapels were built explicitly to provide a separate place for the military monks to worship, so although there are records of shared chapels and parochial spaces in England, it would be very curious if this were the only Christian space available to the residents of Galway until well into the fourteenth century.[13] In fact, the only 'evidence' for a Templar presence there is the dubious identification of a circular foundation shown on the well-known seventeenth-century pictorial map outside the east gate.[14] Traditionally, the Templars built circular chapels emulating the form of the church of the Holy Sepulchre at Jerusalem, and it may be that the maker of the map misunderstood what was more likely a distinctly Irish remnant of a ring fort for a building of more exotic origin. The tradition of a Templar presence in Galway may have led to the mis-attribution of the thirteenth-century grave-slab now in the chapel of Christ in St Nicholas' as that of a 'crusader'.[15] Its identification as such is based on the sword-like shape of the floriated cross. However, there is no evidence to link this iconography with the Templars, rather, it appears to be a type common to the latter part of the thirteenth century in Connacht, with similar designs found, for example, at Athenry friary.[16]

The proposed existence of an earlier chapel dedicated to St Nicholas is more plausible. Nicholas was patron saint of merchant mariners, and Irish churches and chapels dedicated to him can be traced back to the eleventh century.[17] In scantily populated ports, merchants sometimes founded their own stand-alone chapels to cater for their spiritual needs, but typically only when there was no parish church nearby.[18] The earliest documentary evidence for a chapel as opposed to a church dedicated to St Nicholas in Galway is for 1420, in a bequest '*ad fabricam capell[a] Sancti Nicholay [...] ville de Galvy*', however, it is unclear whether this refers to a chapel in a larger church or a separate stand-alone structure, as no reference is made to its precise location.[19]

The only chapel for which there is a clear record prior to the early fourteenth-century ecclesiastical taxation is linked to the hospital or hospice of St Mary on the western bank of the mouth of the River Corrib established by the Ó hAllmhuráin (O'Halloran) family in 1235 as a dependency of the abbey of the Holy Trinity in Tuam.[20] This is discussed further below.

2. God and Mammon: politics and the parish

PARISH CHURCHES IN ANGLO-NORMAN TOWNS

Already by 1247 and 1266 the settlement at Galway was described as a 'town'. The scale of the settlement at these points is impossible to gauge, but the grant of murage in 1272 suggests the establishment of a chartered seignorial borough by that date and, with it, a planned urban space.[1] While the pastoral needs of a lordly retinue or modest population might be catered for in a castle chapel or chapel of ease, the establishment of a borough nearly always incorporated a parish church. For example, in Kilkenny, a chapel dedicated to St Mary, originally built to serve the 1170s castle, was substantially rebuilt around 1200 by William Marshal, earl of Pembroke and lord of Leinster, as the principal parish church of Kilkenny's Hightown. Set within a 0.5ha precinct, it had a long chancel, transepts and an aisled nave, its cemetery providing the main burial place for the populace of the new town.[2] At New Ross, the same patron's son is credited with the construction of an equally ambitious church. St Michael's (later St Mary's) had an aisled nave and transepts from the time of its construction in c.1220–5.[3] Similarly, at Carrickfergus, construction of St Nicholas' Church is usually credited to John de Courcy, its construction dateable to the decades immediately following the construction of his castle there in the late 1170s.[4]

Surviving parish churches from this period are typically relatively modest single- or two-cell structures with aisleless naves.[5] The notable exceptions are churches in newly established boroughs that were, or were soon to become, major centres of trade. In addition to those mentioned above, St Mary's, Youghal (c.1250), and St Multose, Kinsale (rebuilt on the site of an earlier Romanesque church c.1200–50), also had aisled naves and transepts from the outset.[6] This was likely the case in St Peter's, Drogheda, and St Nicholas', Dundalk, too, although subsequent rebuilding and a lack of early documentation mean there is no definitive evidence of this.[7]

The extra space required in a port church was not solely to cater for larger congregation sizes participating in the sacraments and hebdomadal worship. Until the fourteenth century, churches and churchyards provided a common setting for trade and commerce. The physical and the spiritual protection afforded by the parish church also provided ideal conditions for the storage of possessions as well as affording sanctuary to fugitives and felons. Court proceedings relating to a theft from St Michael's church, Athy, in 1311, for example, reveal the presence of chests belonging to eight private individuals that had contained commodities as diverse as silver, bacon, fabric, beans and clothing.[8] This was a role fulfilled by friary and monastery churches too, particularly in areas that lacked other secure structures.[9]

The church also provided an important place for both local and visiting merchants to offer their final prayers for safety before departure, and of thanksgiving for a safe arrival.[10] The range of relatively exotic dedications of intramural parish churches in Dublin implies that in some cases merchants of a particular ethnicity worshiped in dedicated chapels that later came to be absorbed into parish churches.[11] More overarching provision for an explicitly mercantile community is indicated by dedications to St Nicholas, patron saint of merchants. Irish churches and chapels dedicated to him can be traced back to the eleventh century at a number of significant ports and trading centres including Carrickfergus, Dundalk, Dublin (two churches), Clonmines, Limerick and Galway.

THE ESTABLISHMENT OF A PARISH CHURCH IN GALWAY

The earliest church on the site of St Nicholas' may have started life as a church or chapel impropriate to Abbeyknockmoy. The origins of the dedication are unknown but, as noted above, it was not unusual to find chapels for seafarers dedicated to the saint at ports, often separate to a parish church.[12] However, it would be extraordinary if the de Burghs had not embellished the building that was so central (both physically and metaphorically) to the burgeoning town at some point between the erection of their first castle in the 1230s and the walling of the town in the 1270s. The growth and wealth of the town by the turn of the thirteenth and fourteenth centuries also implies that there would have been a practical, spiritual and symbolic requirement for a church of some scale.

By 1290, Galway is estimated to have ranked among the top ten largest urban centres in the country, as success of its port continued to grow.[13] Although its population was unlikely to have exceeded two thousand, it was large enough to support a Franciscan community, with a house established there by 1296. Ranking seventh in Ireland in terms of customs revenue, there would have been more than enough wealth flowing through the town to support a parish church of some scale. This is confirmed in the taxation assessments of the ecclesiastical income completed in Ireland for the diocese of Tuam (then recently amalgamated with Annaghdown).[14] Analysis of these records by Chris Chevalier demonstrates that returns in Connacht, which were directly based on the wealth of parishes, were disproportionately higher in areas over which the de Burghs had authority, notably Galway, Athenry and Loughrea.[15]

That Galway had a parish church of some scale by the turn of the thirteenth and fourteenth centuries seems a given. Hidden beneath multiple layers of subsequent expansion and rebuilding of the current church, however, its exact form is difficult to extract. The clearest indication of its development is reflected in the pattern of its exterior masonry walls. Jim McKeon noted that the lowest courses of masonry in parts of the chancel and two transepts of St Nicholas' were similar in material and pattern to surviving parts of the town walls and the foundations of the de Burgh's hall.[16] This indicates the potential existence of a transeptal church in the town in the thirteenth century, the transepts of sufficient length to accommodate an aisled nave. The walls of the chancel are considerably thicker than those of the transepts, perhaps an indication that it was originally vaulted, but more likely that it represents an earlier building on the site, to which transepts and nave were added.[17] The original form of this earliest structure may never be fully recoverable, but it is of note that the east wall of the space behind the current organ is of a similar depth to the chancel. This may relate to the space identified on the seventeenth-century pictorial map as 'the altar of St Patrick, in the chapel dedicated to him *since the earliest times* [our italics]'; record perhaps of a folk memory of the pre-Anglo-Norman activity on the site.[18]

GALWAY AND CONFLICT WITH THE ARCHDIOCESE OF TUAM

The papal taxation of 1303–6 reveals that the town of Galway supported both a rectory and a vicariate.[19] From 1327, the town was served by vicars or curates appointed by the Cistercians of Abbeyknockmoy and approved or licensed by the archbishops of Tuam. This displeased the townspeople, who were conscious of their English identity and allegiances and who chafed at being under Gaelic ecclesiastical authority. In *c.*1385 the townspeople protested to Pope Urban VI about the situation but, despite some concessions, the right of appointment remained with the Cistercians. In 1398/9 the townspeople again appealed to Rome for relief and Pope Boniface IX decreed that Galway should be established as a perpetual vicariate governed by clerics acceptable to and appointed by its citizens.[20] The first of these to be nominated was John Lang, a priest of the diocese of Cashel, but it is unclear whether he gained possession. The decision was contested by the Cistercians, who received support from the archbishop of Tuam and the fifteenth-century papal registers contain numerous references to disputes over appointments to the church in Galway.

ERECTION OF THE WARDENSHIP IN GALWAY

The appointment of Donatus Ó Muireadhaigh (O'Murray) as archbishop of Tuam in 1450 proved decisive in the ecclesiastical affairs of Galway. As a former vicar of Galway himself, he had first-hand experience of the town's unique situation. It was also during his episcopate that the dioceses of Annaghdown and Tuam were finally united, and Galway passed definitively to the territory of the latter. This development presumably provided the context for the townspeople to seek greater ecclesiastical independence, even as they sought more municipal autonomy. Thus, on 28 September 1484, in response to their appeal, Archbishop Ó Muireadhaigh erected the church of St Nicholas as a collegiate establishment enjoying exemption from the ordinary jurisdiction of Tuam. This arrangement was confirmed by Pope Innocent VIII in the bull *Super Dominicum gregem* issued on 8 September 1485.[21] The college was to consist of eight priests or vicars presided over by a warden who enjoyed ordinary jurisdiction over church affairs and was responsible for the pastoral care of the parishioners. The eight vicars were to assist him in exercising pastoral ministry and were to ensure a high standard of liturgical observance in their daily celebrations of the Eucharist and the Divine Office according to 'English decency'. They were also expected to be exemplary in learning and morals so as to better serve the parishioners of St Nicholas, 'modest and civil people who live surrounded by walls, not following the customs of the mountainous and wild people of those parts'.[22]

The warden and vicars were to be elected each August by the mayor and corporation. The warden was to present himself for re-election annually, but the election of the vicars occurred only when there was a vacancy. The archbishop of Tuam retained some rights of visitation over the parish, though these were not clearly defined, and this became an ongoing cause of contention. Although the warden enjoyed quasi-episcopal authority, he could not ordain clerics and so the town was ultimately reliant on the archbishops for its clergy. To secure this new arrangement financially, Archbishop Ó Muireadhaigh assigned to the wardenship the revenues of the parishes of St Nicholas, Galway, and St James, Claregalway. In addition, he endowed it with other incomes that he enjoyed from the town of Galway along with some other endowments and benefices.

Ó Muireadhaigh's successor as archbishop of Tuam, Uilliam Seóighe [William Joyce], was another native of Galway who continued his predecessor's policy of supporting the new institution by confirming its existing possessions and increasing its endowments. On 8 December 1485 the churches of Oranmore and Maree were assigned to the wardenship. On 23 January 1488 the parish of Oughterard was added to the portfolio while on 12 April 1488 the parish church of St Mary, Rahoon, was also assimilated. The church of Skryne in the episcopal city of Tuam was transferred on 8 February 1491 and the parish of Shrule, also within Tuam diocese, joined to it on 17 August 1501. The final territorial expansion occurred sometime before 1526 when the parish of Roscam was aggregated to the wardenship.[23] These arrangements did not go uncontested, and a number of papal bulls survive confirming the transfers and silencing opponents of the new entity. By 1529, however, litigation over the wardenship's parochial possessions had ceased, at least temporarily.[24]

The mayor and corporation maintained a keen interest in the church affairs of Galway. The unique structure of the wardenship gave the town fathers unprecedented influence in ecclesiastical affairs that they frequently exercised.[25] In 1489, 1506 and 1542 they petitioned successive archbishops of Tuam for confirmation of grants conceded by their predecessors. They also enacted legislation to oversee the college, secure its income and regulate the life of its clerics.

In 1557, a set of comprehensive statutes was enacted that probably encapsulate earlier legislation.[26] These instructed that the daily celebration of the Divine Office in church by the warden and priests of the college should include the 'small hours' of Terce, Sext and None. As this was supplementary to the morning services of Matins and Lauds and the evening celebrations of Vespers and Compline, it meant that the collegiate clergy were committed to an intense regime of corporate liturgical worship. The statutes also provided for four boy choristers to assist at the liturgy and particularly at the singing of the daily 'Mary Mass', a popular medieval devotion in honour of the Blessed Virgin and one which would have been celebrated on weekdays in the church's Lady Chapel and at the high altar in the choir on Saturdays.[27]

As with the warden and vicars themselves, the choristers were appointed by the mayor and corporation as vacancies arose and the college community was responsible for their education and maintenance. If it failed in this, the mayor reserved the right to levy a fine on its income. The warden and vicars were expected to maintain a communal lifestyle and not to use the common fund to improve individual accommodation. An instruction that vicars should not be out at night without good reason echoes an ordinance of 1520 that forbade any 'priest, monk, canon or friar' from maintaining a mistress or concubine in any house in the town.[28] In 1530 it was also decreed that a college priest would be subject to a fine of one hundred shillings and deprived of his position if he was found guilty of any crime or of impregnating anyone.[29] The members of the college were also forbidden from appealing to the archbishop of Tuam in the event of a dispute as this was prejudicial to the authority of the mayor and corporation who maintained the right to correct their 'disobediance, evill demeanours, or naughty procedings'.[30]

The civic authorities also committed themselves to the temporal welfare of the church and its clergy. Within a month of his election to office, the mayor was obliged to examine the proctors' or churchwardens' accounts along with those of the town's Franciscan friary. The corporation also ensured that the collection of tithes of grain was enforced, and an ordinance of 1517 decreed that any fishing crew taking 'fyre, watter or service' in Galway had to pay a half tithe of the catch to the college clergy. One third of all fines levied in Galway were allocated to the maintenance of the church fabric and, along with the mayor and bailiffs, the warden had first choice on any meat or fish offered for sale within the town.[31] The tithe revenues of the collegiate church must have been considerable, particularly after they had been augmented by the income from the various parishes aggregated to the wardenship between 1485 and 1526.

In addition, the warden and vicars customarily enjoyed other sources of income, which were listed in an inquisition conducted in 1609.[32] The town's blacksmiths, brass makers, carpenters, fishermen, glovers, weavers, goldsmiths, hoopers, joiners, masons, potters, shoemakers, tailors and tinkers each had to pay five shillings towards the repairs of the church before they could start practising their craft. The town's bakers and chandlers, who enjoyed a monopoly on their trade, each had to pay five shillings annually to secure their rights. Brewers of ale paid twelve pence annually in lieu of a bottle of beer from every brewing, while distillers of whiskey were liable for the value of one pint for every four gallons offered for sale. Ships entering the harbour paid one penny for each ton of their cargo, which increased to two pence per ton for more valuable commodities like honey, iron, salt and wine. At Easter, each merchant or freeman paid dues to the value of four pence for each member of his family, while labourers and their households paid two pence per head. Bachelors were levied at two pence as well.

Masons, glaziers and labourers working on the repair of the parish church were provided with sustenance by the merchants and gentry of the town, though the warden and vicars were obliged to give the glaziers their breakfast daily and to provide for the support of one mason. The fabric fund of the church also benefitted from rents accruing from the houses and properties bequeathed to it by deceased citizens.[33] In addition to these obligations, many other parishioners expressed their devotion by voluntary donations to the church and its fabric. This is particularly evident in the late medieval additions to the church, through which the merchants of the town vied with each other to produce concrete expressions of piety, prestige and civic pride.

3. Experiencing the medieval church

Whereas the great building projects of the thirteenth century were typically instigated by noble newcomers, the following century saw a notable shift towards mercantile patrimony, particularly in urban areas. It was around the same time that the focus of commercial activity in the church and churchyard also began to shift, prompted initially by crown legislation and, latterly, through synodal decree forbidding all business, including the hearing of lawsuits, holding of fairs or the erection of secular buildings within churches or cemeteries.[1]

It was in the early decades of the fourteenth century that the first unambiguous records of the erection of market crosses and tholsel/market houses appear, marking the decoupling of the church and commerce in a more physical way.[2] The shift was not absolute, however, and a strong relationship was maintained between the two, with market places typically located in proximity to the parish church, as was, and still is the case at Galway.[3] The funding of church fabric was frequently linked to trade. In addition to the provisions outlined above, other examples include St Mary's, Kilkenny, where the corporation collected four pence from each hall (house) and a halfpenny from each stall or shop annually for maintenance of the church and used both it and its tower for corporation meetings.[4] At Waterford, ships carrying merchandise to Flanders were obliged to deliver 'God's penny' towards the maintenance of the cathedral before sailing.[5]

The requirements of the parish church also evolved. As populations grew, so too did the demand for burial space. Where wealth permitted, the preferred spot was within the church building, as close as possible to the areas of greatest ritual; in front of or to the south of the high altar or, in lieu of this, adjacent to a minor altar or

favoured devotional image. Popular cults, such as that of the Virgin
Mary, prompted the construction of new, dedicated chapels within
the sacred space. Some were set aside as chantries, where individual
families funded prayers for their salvation, others were established by
guilds formed by those who shared a trade or particular devotion. It
was during this century too, that there was a notable move towards
the construction of church towers.[6] The ringing of bells was essential
to call an ever-expanding urban population to work, to prayer, to
mark solemn occasions and to commemorate the dead. In coastal
locations, church towers also played an important navigational role as
well as providing a first impression of the standing of a town to the
approaching visitor.

THE DEVELOPMENT OF THE FABRIC

It is in this context that around 1320 the 'body' of the church,
possibly already a building of some scale, was rebuilt under the
patronage of the Lynches.[7] The 'body' typically referred to the nave,
the western part of the church for which the congregation and its
representatives, the churchwardens, were responsible, and were liable
for citation and penalty if they failed in this duty.[8] The entire outer
shell of St Nicholas' nave has been altered by additions, and so it is
only part of the north nave arcade and the three westernmost bays
of the south arcade that might now be said, tentatively, to represent
an early fourteenth-century intervention in this part of the building.[9]
Other incidental documentary sources suggest that the west front
was framed by pinnacles at the north and south corners, lost with the
subsequent lateral expansion of the aisles. Also lost are the windows.
Datable examples of near-contemporary re-glazing at Tuam
Cathedral and Athenry Priory, however, suggest that they were
created using light, cusped bars that formed circled or foiled openings
in the upper registers of the windows – the so-called 'geometric' style
favoured in England at the time.[10] These introduced a larger field for
glazing than had hitherto been possible in the narrower lancets more
typical of the thirteenth century.

There is no direct evidence for a crossing tower at St Nicholas'
until the fifteenth century, but this does not exclude the possibility
that one was incorporated in the 1320s building programme. Where

1. Plan of St Nicholas' Collegiate Church, Galway.

1. Rood screen
2. High altar of St Nicholas
3. Altar of Christ Judging
4. Altar of St Michael
5. Altar of St Mary Major
6. Altar of the Blessed Virgin Mary

7. Altar of St James
8. Altar of St Catherine
9. Altar of St John the Baptist
10. Altar of the Holy Trinity
11. Altar of St Patrick
12. Altar of St Anne

13. Altar of St Bridget
14. Altar of the Blessed Sacrament
15. Altar of St Martin
16. Font
17a&b. Primary and secondary locations of the Lynch tomb.

Modern

later towers were added to early parish churches, they were typically located at the west end, thus minimizing disruption to the existing fabric of the church.[11] Given its port location, and the fashion for tower building across Ireland at the time, the incorporation of a crossing tower then would have been logical. Though rare, this would not be without precedent in Ireland, for example the thirteenth- and fourteenth-century parish church at Gowran, commissioned by the powerful Butler earls of Ormond, had a crossing tower from the outset.

Like many churches, cathedrals and religious houses in late medieval Ireland, the church of St Nicholas in Galway was extensively refurbished and extended in the fifteenth and sixteenth centuries.[12] The widening of the eastern two bays of the north aisle and addition of a lateral chapel to this may have occurred in the late fourteenth or early fifteenth centuries. In 1484–5, the transformation of the church from a vicarage to a collegiate foundation instigated more major works, including the enlargement of the entire south aisle, addition of a new south porch and the heightening of the choir. Further additions in the sixteenth century included the expansion of the westernmost bays of the nave in *c*.1538 by Mayor John French and the extension of the south transept to accommodate a new mortuary chapel for the Lynch family (fig. 1).

These works were emblematic of the town's remarkable social, political, economic and religious expansion under the leadership of its merchant oligarchy, whose heraldry and merchant marks were carved indelibly into the fabric of the church and its monuments.[13]

ST NICHOLAS': LITURGY AND LIFE

By decree of the mayor and corporation, the liturgy celebrated in St Nicholas' followed the 'customs of the English church'. This referred to the liturgical norms of the church of Salisbury, otherwise known as the Use of Sarum.[14] These had been adopted throughout Ireland from the twelfth century onwards. The Sarum liturgy was a variant or 'use' of the Roman rite and was famous for its precision and elaborate ceremonial, which, by the late fifteenth century, had undergone thorough revision and standardization. It was particularly noteworthy for the number of liturgical processions that it featured. Provision was made for up to one hundred of these in the course of the liturgical year. Most of these occurred within the church itself and included the weekly blessing and sprinkling of holy water before the principal Mass on Sundays, a procession to the rood each Friday and to the shrines and altars of the saints on their feast days. Other devotions, such as the annual *Corpus Christi*, Palm Sunday and Rogationtide processions, spilled out onto the streets and involved the whole community in a display of civic devotion and unity. The illustration of a large churchyard cross on the seventeenth-century pictorial map indicates that it formed a station on the annual Palm Sunday procession. The presence of a corps of well-trained clergy and choirboys from the 1480s meant that the parishioners of Galway would have been accustomed to a high standard of liturgical music and ceremonial.[15]

The late medieval architecture of St Nicholas', still relatively intact today, provides testament to the architectural framework for these processions and other liturgies.

THE DOORWAYS AND PORCH

In addition to its practical function, the doorway of a medieval church embodied several symbolic functions.[16] It demarcated the transition from secular to sacred space, from the world of men to the realm of God. The principal doorway of a church was the place where some of the most important events in the life of a Christian occurred. Generally situated in the west gable, it was here that the priest conducted the first part of the baptismal liturgy, the admission to the catechumenate. Women were also greeted at the church door when they came to be churched after childbirth.[17] The preliminaries of the wedding ceremony took place *in facie ecclesiae* to ensure the maximum number of witnesses for the ceremony, while at the funeral liturgy the reception of the corpse occurred here before it was borne into the church. In consequence, the western doorway was often highly decorated. This is the case at St Nicholas', where a delicately moulded doorway with pinnacles was inserted in the late fifteenth century.[18] It was used for ceremonial and processional activities during the high points of the liturgical year such as *Corpus Christi* and Palm Sunday, or for the formal reception of civic dignitaries and distinguished visitors.

In addition to the ceremonial west entrance, there are opposing doorways in the north and south walls of St Nicholas', and these probably provided separate entrances for male and female worshippers to access the sections of the church they habitually occupied during services, with women on the north side and men on the south. In the Sarum liturgy, the north doorway was used for the ceremonial expulsion of penitents at the start of Lent. The south doorway at St Nicholas' remains the primary entrance and is protected by a two-storey porch that, in addition to sheltering participants in the ceremonies outlined above, provided a venue where beggars could gather and shelter for those seeking sanctuary. Porches patronized by specific, named, donors in the early sixteenth century are recorded at Rathmore in Co. Meath and at Galway, where its construction is credited to sometime mayor, Dominic *Dubh* Lynch, founder of the college (d. 1508).[19] The vestry minutes of the parish of St Werburgh's, Dublin, refer to 'the lityll chamber ofver the church dore' as the residence of a chaplain, and it is likely that the upper storey of the porch at St Nicholas' served a similar function.[20] At a later stage in its history, this upper room functioned as the muniments room for the corporation records.[21]

THE FONT

From the twelfth century the font in the parish church became the normal place for baptism. Fonts were normally situated in the south-west corner of the church as is the case in St Nicholas'. This had both symbolic and practical aspects. Positioned adjacent to the main entrance of the church, it symbolically reiterated that one entered the Christian community through the rite of baptism. Being located off-centre meant that it did not interfere with any of the processions that took place on the major feast days of the liturgical year. In Ireland, where stone examples survive from the twelfth century onwards, the shape of the font varies, with circular, square and rectangular bowls more common in the twelfth to fourteenth centuries, and the symbolic octagonal form becoming more popular from the fifteenth.[22] The St Nicholas' font is roughly square, so of an earlier form, but its decoration betrays a late fifteenth-century date. This comprises flowing window tracery designs and floral motifs. The carving of three fleur-de-lis and small, four-legged creature on the east face have sometimes been mistaken for the Lynch heraldry (three shamrocks and a chevron, their badge is a lynx). The decoration of fonts with arcades or architectural designs at that time was quite common. For example, designs on the fonts at Johnstown Church (formerly Fertagh), Kilkenny and Kilcooly Abbey in Tipperary come from the pattern books of the so-called O'Tunney atelier and reflect forms found in some of their full-scale window tracery and vaulting designs.[23] While the designs on the Galway font cannot be found in surviving local window tracery, they do reflect a similar style to the windows of the south aisle, so the font was most likely made, or refurbished around the same time – the end of the fifteenth century. In the Sarum liturgy the blessing of the waters of the font was an elaborate ceremony that occurred as part of the Easter Vigil on Holy Saturday and care was taken to protect the consecrated water from becoming contaminated or being used for nefarious purposes by providing the font with a lockable cover, as is evident in the St Nicholas' example.

THE NAVE

The western part of the church building was reserved primarily for the laity. It was the place where the congregation stood and knelt during celebrations of the Eucharist and the Divine Office on Sundays and feast days, where they gathered for baptisms, marriages and funerals and where they observed the clergy in the frequent processions that characterized the Sarum liturgy.

From the twelfth century the nave was increasingly demarcated from the preserve of the clergy in the choir and chancel through the use of screens, rood lofts and other architectural features. These were typically constructed of timber and so no longer survive, although a number of decorated limestones slabs, eight of which were re-set in the so-called 'leper gallery' between 1958 and 1962, may once have formed part of a more permanent stone partition in the church.[24]

TRANSEPTS, CHAPELS AND SIDE ALTARS

Although the majority of medieval Irish parish churches possessed only one altar (the high altar situated at the east end of the chancel under the great east window), it was common for churches served by a number of priests (such as monasteries, friaries and collegiate foundations like St Nicholas') to have additional minor altars situated throughout the building. Local merchants, gentry or guilds sponsored these to function as chantries where Mass was offered daily for the donors' intentions and for the repose of the souls of their deceased members and ancestors. These chantry chapels often functioned as family mausoleums. In addition to providing an income to support the chantry priest, benefactors also donated the necessary liturgical vestments, altar vessels, books and other accoutrements. These frequently bore inscriptions or heraldic devices that acted both as mementos and as statements of dynastic prestige. The altars' dedications often reflected the donors' piety and acted as a focus for particular devotions and saints' cults.[25] The clergy who served these chantries also assisted at the parochial liturgy at the high altar and in choir, which was thereby enhanced by the presence of more ministers. They were likewise expected to educate local children and to oversee the charitable and administrative work of the parish.

St Nicholas' is the best documented example of this development in Ireland, as the late medieval expansion of the church provided space for these chapels and the presence of thirteen ancillary altars is recorded in the commentary of the mid-seventeenth-century pictorial map.[26] This also gives the dedication of each altar and so provides a snapshot of the devotional world of late medieval Galway. The principal or high altar in the choir of the church was dedicated to the patron, St Nicholas of Myra.

The south transept ultimately housed either three or four chapels and functioned as the mausoleum of the Lynch family. According to the pictorial map, the first of these, at 'the right of the entrance to the choir', was dedicated to Jesus Christ in judgment. The reference to 'judgment' may indicate that this chapel held a depiction of the Doom or 'Last Judgment' with Christ in majesty condemning the damned and rewarding the just, perhaps similar to the carving of the Judging Christ on the Lynch tomb, a distinctive iconography that also places emphasis on Christ's five wounds.[27] It was possibly the location of a Christocentric cult like the 'Jesus Mass' or the 'Mass of the Five Wounds', discussed below. Its exact location is uncertain, but may have been under the rood, so at the very northern end of the transept, or possibly in an eastern projecting structure in the space now occupied by the 'Peace Chapel'.[28] Prior to the southern extension of the transept in 1561, the area in front of this chapel accommodated the Mary chapel, ancestral burial place of the Lynches. It is most likely the original location of the flamboyant wall monument with its carved image of the Judging Christ, now located farther south in the later extension. Wall tombs of this type are more commonly found in the late fifteenth and early sixteenth centuries; the distinctive iconography of the Christ figure also finds its closest parallels at this time and it may be the tomb that Edmund Lynch (d. 1462), 'venerable burgess of Galway' and sovereign of the town in 1434 and 1443, commissioned for himself and 'his own' in the 'chapel of the Blessed Virgin in the parish church of Galway'.[29] The presence of a burial vault in the northern part of the transept (in front on the Peace Chapel) suggests that this tomb once occupied this space, marking the presence of the family vault below. This is comparable to the slightly later Rothe wall monument and vault in the north transept, or chapel of St Michael, at St Mary's, Kilkenny.[30] At Galway, the monument would have doubled as the altar of the Blessed Mary, which the Lynches felt compelled to relocate as their chapel migrated southwards.

The description of the next altar, dedicated to St Michael 'in the chapel of the angels', may reference the now mutilated faces of the stone angels bearing lights that flanked the altar beneath the window. This chapel was founded by William Lynch (d. 1492), who, as provost of Galway, had overseen the elevation of the church to collegiate status.[31] St Michael presided at the Last Judgment and the guardian angels did battle with demons at a Christian's deathbed over the fate of the soul. They were therefore appropriate intercessors for deceased benefactors.

By 1560 and following the introduction of the Book of Common Prayer the way the church buildings were used to celebrate the liturgy slowly began to change.[32] 'Prayer book' worship was moved to the more inclusive body of the church, with regular sermons preached from the pulpit. However, change was gradual, and one particularly enduring aspect was the long tradition of familial burial in the church. Families who remained faithful to the 'old religion' were confronted with the dilemma of wishing to continue the tradition of interment with their ancestors but faced with the fact that this now entailed burial in a Reformed church.

St Nicholas' contains evidence of a common solution to the problem. In 1561, Nicholas Lynch FitzStephen commissioned the extension of the south transept – his old family chapel. The commission included an organ and a bell and a stair tower to which only family members held a key.[33] The extent of the new structure is clearly evident in a change of masonry styles on the exterior of the building. The new chapel, dedicated to the Virgin Mary, saw the relocation of the wall tomb, referred to in the seventeenth-century map as the altar of St Mary Major. Beyond this is the highly decorated base of a stone structure in the south-east corner, referred to as the 'altar of the Blessed [Virgin] Mary in the new large chapel of the Blessed [Virgin] Mary'. This probably represents the base of a cage chantry similar to that of the earl of Kildare in Dublin's Christ Church Cathedral, which, like the Lynch monument, was richly adorned with the arms of family and allies.[34] A stone frame above the tomb base once housed a devotional image or painting. Alternatively, it may have displayed a list of the indulgences available to those who visited the chapel, contributed to its upkeep and prayed for those buried there. A puzzling feature of the structure is its orientation. Unlike the church, it is orientated closer to due east. This creates an awkward junction between the structure and transept walls, as if to infer that it was an existing structure clumsily subsumed by the later church. The structure would originally have been enclosed and contained a tomb and altar and was accessed by steps. The window arrangement in the transept makes clear that there was originally a gallery at the southern end of the transept. This was accessed directly from the churchyard via the external stair tower, so providing a private view into the transept that enabled the Lynches access, without having to pass through the church.

The south aisle, extended southwards by Nicholas Lynch FitzStephen's grandfather, Mayor Dominic *Dubh* Lynch, and his son Stephen housed altars dedicated to SS James, Catherine of Alexandria and John the Baptist. The chapel of St James was begun by Dominic *Dubh* (d. 1508), who left instructions in his will for its completion.[35] Situated at the south aisle column nearest the chapel of the Blessed Virgin, its dedication indicates the popularity of the cult of the Apostle James in medieval Galway and of the well-documented tradition of pilgrimage to Compostela from the town discussed below. The chapel of St Catherine of Alexandria was located at the east end of the aisle. Peter Lynch (d. 1507), brother of Dominic *Dubh*, was founder of the chapel in 1494, funding a chaplain to pray for him and his wife, Ellen Blake, there.[36] He was buried in front of the altar.[37] The reference to a 'gilt chapel' in the pictorial map indicates that, although established by an individual, it was a focus of devotion for a guild in the parish. The dedication of guilds to St Catherine was common and has been linked to her as a symbol of authority and power, making her a popular choice for guilds closely associated with local government.[38]

St John the Baptist was regarded as the greatest of the saints after the Virgin Mary and inspired widespread devotion. His altar was probably located near the irregularly shaped column on the south side of the nave, opposite St Catherine's chapel, which may also have been the location of the church's pulpit.

The north transept of the church housed the altar of St Anne and this dedication complemented the dedication of the south transept to her daughter, the Virgin Mary. The chapel of St Patrick was located in an eastern extension to the north transept, which, as noted above, incorporates some of the older fabric of the church. In 1420 John Óg Blake left a bequest to the fabric of the chapel of St Anne.[39] The bequest of another Blake, John FitzWilliam, in 1468, for the celebration of masses at the altar of St Patrick, suggests that this area was a favoured chantry or burial place for that family at the time.[40] The Holy Trinity chapel, located 'under the organ', may have been situated under the rood, as one entered the chancel and may have possessed an image of the Throne of Mercy similar to those that survive from the Dominican Black Abbey in Kilkenny or from the parish church in Fethard, Co. Tipperary. These depict God the Father cradling the crucified Christ with the Holy Spirit in the form of a dove completing the tableau.[41]

The north aisle of the church accommodated altars and chapels dedicated to SS Bridget, Martin of Tours and to the Blessed Sacrament. The altar to St Bridget at the 'northern column' may refer to the column marking transition from aisle into transept. The Blessed Sacrament chapel occupied a projecting northern annex to the aisle.

Harold Leask took the eastern part of the north nave aisle to be the extension built by John French, recorded in 1538, implying these two chapels' establishment after that date.[42] However, his analysis of the church fabric to support this claim is not convincing and neither does it fit comfortably with the religious climate of the time. The Anglican reformation, enacted in 1536, was slow to take hold in Galway, but by 1538 some devotional images were evidently removed from the church in advance of a visit from Lord Deputy Grey.[43] The founding of an altar to St Bridget, with attendant devotional images to the saint, after this date seems very unlikely. Similarly, as this was the very time when the eucharistic doctrine of transubstantiation fell under disapproval, such a late and prominent dedication of a chapel to the Blessed Sacrament is unconvincing.[44]

St Martin of Tours, whose altar was situated beside the north door of the church, was a fourth-century soldier who became a monk and bishop. One of the most popular of the medieval saints, he was the saintly patron of vintners and viticulture and his cult may reflect the importance of the wine trade for the town's merchants. As the index to the pictorial map suggests that the altars were no longer in place in the seventeenth century, it is unclear whether this altar was positioned by the old north door, or the new one created when this part of the church was extended by John French in 1538. Either way, it is tempting to associate it with one of the other prominent mercantile families of the time, the Martins.

THE ROOD SCREEN

The rood screen in St Nicholas' occupied the western arch of the crossing and probably consisted of a substantial wooden structure that incorporated a loft and above which the church's crucifix (or rood) was displayed, flanked by images of the Virgin Mary and St John the Beloved Disciple. The rood screen dominated the interiors of most medieval parish churches. It demarcated the space reserved for the clergy from that of the laity and provided a physical and psychological barrier between the nave and the chancel where the sacred rite of the Eucharist was performed. A generous bequest of £5 from Dominic *Dubh* Lynch, made for repair of the 'holy cross' in the church, may refer to repairs to the rood.[45]

THE BELFRY AND BELLS

As noted above, crossing towers in medieval Irish parish churches are unusual, and it is possible that a tower at St Nicholas' was erected as part of the rebuilding of the nave in the 1320s. The detailing of the stout supporting piers is coeval with the building programme

undertaken by the Lynches in the southern part of the church from
the 1480s, but the lack of reference to it in the otherwise copiously
documented examples of their generosity is unusual. Alterations were
certainly made to the tower in the late fifteenth century, evidenced
by some of its windows. It may have been this tower that hosted
the bell called Cloghvashine [*Clog bá thine*] 'put forward' in Galway
c.1499/1500 to ring the curfew.[46] A belfry with peal of bells was added
on the tower in 1590 by Mayor James Lynch at a cost of £63.[47]

None of the medieval bells survives at St Nicholas' and in the 1930s
the ring of bells dating from the sixteenth to the nineteenth centuries
was recast.[48] Bells were normally dedicated to a patron saint, and this
was frequently inscribed on the bell itself along with an image of the
saint. Casts of dedication panels survive for some of the St Nicholas'
bells. They depict an Annunciation scene and another image of the
Blessed Virgin and show that at least two of the bells were dedicated
to the Mother of God. The ceremony of blessing a bell in the Sarum
liturgy was closely modelled on the rite of baptism, after which
the bell was believed to 'speak' in the 'voice' of the saint or angel to
whom it had been dedicated. For this reason, bells were rung at times
of celebration and of crisis, they were believed to provide protection
from storms and lightening and to repel the onslaughts of demons in
the form of plagues and diseases. A copy of a medieval bell inscription
from a fifteenth-century Irish Dominican manuscript summarizes
these various functions: 'The nature of a bell: I worship the true God,
I call the people, I gather the clergy together, I intercede for the dead,
repel the plague, I am the terror of all demons'.[49] The regular ringing
of the bells for services and curfews or, less regularly, their tolling to
mark a death or an anniversary would have created a distinctive and
pervasive soundscape for the people of medieval Galway.

THE CROSSING, CHOIR AND CHANCEL

The crossing, choir and chancel area represented the spiritual heart
of St Nicholas' as it did for every medieval church. It was here that
the daily liturgical round of praise, intercession and thanksgiving
took place with the celebration of Mass and the Divine Office. The
choir's central position at the junction of the nave, chancel and

transepts ensured that it received the maximum amount of daylight. The reference in the 1557 statutes that the collegiate clergy were to celebrate the 'small hours' of Terce, Sext and None is an oblique corroboration that the clergy were bound to the public recitation of all the hours of the Divine Office and not just the principal services of Matins and Lauds in the morning and Vespers and Compline in the evening. This was an unusually demanding schedule, comparable to that followed by members of monastic or religious communities. It also contextualizes the decision to re-establish St Nicholas' as a collegiate church in 1484 as a liturgical regime like this required considerable human resources.

The presence of a body of musically trained priests assisted by boy-choristers indicates a high degree of musical attainment and it is likely that the St Nicholas' choristers were capable of part-singing, organum and polyphony in addition to plainchant. The establishment of choral foundations was a feature of a number of Irish collegiate and cathedral foundations in the fifteenth century, including St Patrick's Cathedral, Dublin, Cashel Cathedral and the earl of Kildare's foundation at Maynooth. At Youghal, the chancel of St Mary's Church was rebuilt following the church's transformation to a collegiate foundation in 1464, the incorporation of acoustic vases in the fabric emphasizing the importance of music to the foundation.[50] At Galway, although there is no evidence of an extension to the choir to accommodate more complex liturgical activities, the roof level was raised, perhaps to accommodate an organ or to improve acoustics.

In Britain and Ireland, the choirstalls for the clergy and choristers were generally positioned at the rear of the roodscreen in cathedrals, monastic and collegiate churches, and this is likely to have been the case in Galway. Choir stalls were often elaborate wooden constructions surmounted by ornate canopies, as a surviving seventeenth-century illustration from Christ Church Cathedral demonstrates. As the clergy stood for a good portion of the liturgy, the stalls were equipped with tip-up seats, the undersides of which were provided with small projecting ledges that allowed the cleric to recline. These features, known as misericords, were often decorated with picaresque or grotesque carvings, as is the case with the surviving examples from St Mary's Cathedral in Limerick.

The chancel area or presbytery was reserved for the main daily celebration of the Eucharist. Given the clerical complement available in Galway, it is likely that this consisted of a High Mass with three ministers conducting the service. The bench that they occupied was known as the sedilia and was often an ornate wooden or stone-canopied structure with a tripartite division into seats for the priest, deacon and subdeacon. The niche that the sedilia occupied survives in the south wall of the chancel in St Nicholas', but nothing remains of its medieval fabric. Likewise, no trace survives of the church's medieval high altar or of the Easter sepulchre. Because of their association with the medieval doctrine of eucharistic transubstantiation, Protestant iconoclasts often targeted both these features during the Reformation and relatively few survive intact in Ireland.

The high altar was usually a substantial stone structure situated under the east window of the church. The example that survives from St Mary's Cathedral in Limerick is 4.3m long and weighs 2.7 tonnes. The prominent visibility of the east window and its proximity to the altar created a particularly important canvas for imagery. The 'Account of Galway' for the year 1493 records that James Lynch FitzStephen, mayor that year, 'on his own cost [...] put up all the painted glasses in the Church of St Nicholas'.[51] This would have been the most appropriate medium through which the Lynches could put their corporate stamp on the building, the intense colours providing an appropriate field for heraldic display. Although none of the glass now survives, a fragment of medieval glass bearing the Lynch arms was still displayed in relatively modern times in the east window.[52] Mary O'Sullivan speculated that this is unlikely to have been of local production, indeed there is no evidence of glassmaking in Ireland until the latter part of the sixteenth century.[53] In this context, a record of a shipment of coloured glass from La Rochelle to Limerick and Galway in 1490 provides a clue as to its origins.[54]

4. The ordered life

In addition to the pastoral care provided by the secular clergy of the Collegiate Church of St Nicholas, the citizens of Galway also benefitted from the services of members of the town's male and female mendicant communities.

The Dominicans were the first friars to arrive in Ireland, establishing foundations in Dublin and Drogheda in 1224, while the Franciscans' Irish province was formally erected in 1230. The Carmelite friars are first mentioned in 1271 and the earliest reference to the Augustinians occurs in 1282.[1] During their first wave of expansion, the friars gravitated to the newly established towns and boroughs of the Anglo-Norman colony, but a number of important foundations were also made in Gaelic territories including the Franciscan houses at Ennis and Armagh and a Dominican foundation at Roscommon.

Their arrival coincided with a period of prosperity and expansion in the Anglo-Norman colony and by 1340 the combined orders had established a total of eighty-nine friaries. At the end of the thirteenth century the colony became increasingly beleaguered in the face of climate change, economic downturn, depopulation and Gaelic resurgence. Tensions between the Anglo-Norman and Gaelic members of each order reflected this, particularly among the Franciscans. In 1291, sixteen friars attending the order's provincial chapter in Cork were killed when ethnic tension erupted into violence. The divisions caused by Edward Bruce's Irish campaign (1315–17) exacerbated matters and in 1324, responding to charges made against the Gaelic Franciscans by King Edward II, Pope John XXII appointed the dean of St Patrick's Cathedral, William de Rodierd, as his judge delegate to investigate the complaints. He concluded that the loyalty of eight communities, including Galway and Claregalway, was suspect and instructed that the Gaelic members of these friaries be reassigned to other houses.[2] These 'disloyal' communities formed the nucleus of the Gaelic custody of Nenagh, a constitutional arrangement that copper-fastened the ban on Gaelic friars ever becoming the order's minister provincial in Ireland. Among the Carmelites, Augustinians and Dominicans, rivalry between Anglo-Irish friars and their English major superiors led to conflict that occasionally resulted in physical altercations.[3]

The Black Death (1348–9) had a devastating effect on religious communities, particularly those based in urban environments and port towns. The Kilkenny Franciscan chronicler Friar John Clyn recorded that twenty-five Franciscans died of plague in Drogheda and twenty-three in Dublin before Christmas 1348 and, although no account survives of its impact in Galway, it is likely to have caused similar devastation. As society gradually recovered from the impact of the plague and its subsequent outbreaks, a remarkable efflorescence of the mendicant movement in Ireland occurred in the last decades of the fourteenth century. Unlike the first wave of Anglo-Norman foundations, these new friaries were predominantly established in the Gaelic territories of Connacht and Ulster. Between 1390 and 1510 approximately ninety new houses were established, many as expressions of the strict Observant reform movement that was animating religious life on the Continent and which first emerged among the Irish Dominicans in 1390.[4] This 'back-to-basics' movement stressed the importance of religious discipline, the worthy celebration of the liturgy and individual and corporate asceticism. It proved immensely attractive to patrons who in some cases prevailed on older foundations to accept the reform. It is in this revivalist context that the establishment of two new friaries and at least one nunnery in Galway occurred between 1488 and 1511.

The friars emerged as an energetic papacy sought to renew the Church and its pastoral ministry. This culminated in the Fourth Lateran Council (1215), which established norms for Catholic practice that endured for the rest of the Middle Ages. In particular, the council stressed the importance of regular, or at least annual, reception of communion, which was prepared for by the confession of one's sins. It also stressed the importance of regular preaching and effective catechesis or basic instruction in the Christian faith. The friars, particularly the Dominicans and Franciscans, were swiftly co-opted by the papacy to promote this reform programme and across

Europe their houses provided the network through which texts, ideas and personnel could circulate. Each friary acted as a base from which the friars exercised their ministry as preachers and confessors. Friary churches, with their hall-like naves, side aisles and chapels, were specifically designed as preaching venues for large congregations. Every community was assigned an area within which they were licensed to preach and beg for alms and this brought them into contact with the rural population.

Each friary also functioned as a *studium* and formed part of a sophisticated educational network that provided novices with a basic grounding in the principles of the religious life. Those earmarked for the priesthood received their initial philosophical, theological and pastoral formation from the friary's lector, and brighter candidates were sent to centres for advanced studies either elsewhere in Ireland or abroad.[5] The earliest evidence for a *studium* in the Galway Franciscan friary occurs in 1324 when the lector was transferred by order of Dean William de Rodierd. The Galway *studium* enjoyed considerable standing as in 1438 the provincial, Friar John White, was licensed to establish a centre there for advanced theological studies within the province.[6] As a matter of course, each Dominican community required the presence of a qualified lector before it could be canonically established, and this presumably was the case in Galway. The Dominican *studium* in Athenry had flourished from its foundation in 1241, routinely attracting lectors from England to the extent that a room in the friary was reserved for the 'English Bachelors'. Nor was this one-way traffic: the Athenry necrology records the deaths of Friars Thomas O'Corcoran (d. 1428) and Gilbert Bron (d. 1451), *alumni* of the house, who died in England at the end of distinguished academic careers.[7] Given the close association between the Galway and Athenry foundations, it is probable that the former was equally committed to maintaining high educational standards. Archbishop John Alen of Dublin (d. 1536) maintained that the Dublin Augustinians outshone all others for their learning, but little is known of their arrangements in Galway. Given, however, that Friar Richard Nangle who co-instigated the foundation was described as a professor of theology, it is likely that the community also had the resources to conduct a *studium*.

The primary purpose of the friars was to act as preachers and confessors, thereby augmenting the ministry of the secular clergy.

Although no evidence survives of how they did this in Galway, it is likely that it followed the pattern of their *confrères* elsewhere in Ireland. Regular cycles of sermons would have been preached in the respective friary churches, particularly during the penitential seasons of Lent and Advent when there might have been a daily sermon. The friars also embarked on preaching tours, often during Lent or at harvest time when it was possible for them to solicit alms for their houses as well. The Lenten sermons provided an opportunity to catechize people about worthy reception of the Eucharist at Easter and large numbers of penitents often remained after the friars' sermons to go to confession. Questing for alms was a routine feature of mendicant life and occasionally the source of irritation. In 1523 the mayor was appointed to oversee the accounts of the Franciscan friary and in 1544, as part of a clampdown on various forms of aggressive begging, the corporation decreed that friars were not to enter houses when begging for alms but were to wait outside to receive them.[8]

The high regard in which the friars were held meant that they were often invoked as witnesses or as moral authorities as demonstrated by various muniments and deeds associated with the Blake family of Galway. In 1407, Walter Lawless granted John Blake his share of an eel weir and a tenement in Galway. The transaction took place in the Dominican convent in Sligo and was endorsed by the conventual seal. In 1443, the Franciscan friary in Galway was the scene for a transaction between Henry Blake and his son John whereby the latter gained possession of his father's lands and properties in the town and its environs. The agreement was witnessed by Friar Cornelius, the guardian of the community. Two years later, in 1445, both John and Henry Blake were involved in a dispute with William Blake. Both parties agreed to accept the arbitration of the earl of Clanrickard and Master John, a Dominican of Athenry. Likewise, in 1468, another Athenry Dominican, Friar Henry Joyce, brokered a marriage settlement between Peter Lynch, later first mayor of Galway, and John Blake whose daughter, Evelyn, Lynch wished to marry.[9] The international connections of the friars also worked to the benefit of their benefactors. A late fifteenth-century manuscript from the Franciscan friary in Youghal contains a formulary letter whereby benefactors of the community were introduced to overseas houses of the order with the request that they be offered hospitality and assistance with their merchandise.[10] The various friaries in Galway offered similar assistance to merchants, a practice that led to conflict with the corporation in 1515.[11]

The 1235 invasion of Connacht spearheaded by Richard de Burgh and Maurice FitzGerald provided the impetus for the mendicants' westward expansion. Dominican foundations were established by Maurice FitzGerald at Sligo (1253), by Miler de Bermingham at Athenry (1241) and by members of the Dexter family at Strade (1252) and Rathfran (1274).[12] John de Cogan II founded a Franciscan friary at Claregalway before 1252 and William de Burgh established their house in Galway in 1296.[13] The Carmelite and Augustinian friars each made one foundation in Connacht. Sometime around 1300, Richard de Burgh, earl of Ulster, founded a Carmelite friary at Loughrea, Co. Galway, while Lady Elizabeth de Clare established the Augustinian friars at Ballinrobe, Co. Mayo, c.1312.[14]

Galway's first exposure to the mendicant orders was in 1296, with the foundation of the Franciscan friary on St Stephen's Island to the east of the town by William de Burgh. The seventeenth-century pictorial map shows the Franciscan friary church with a northern cloister and a southern transept, typical of the order in Ireland (fig. 2). The conventual buildings are shown as still intact at that time – with the cloister and dormitory apparently fully roofed. The latter was most likely the dormitory that had been built in the late fifteenth century by Edmund McPhilbin.[15] John French's 'great chapel on the south side of the abbey' built in 1538, the same year as he extended the north aisle of St Nicholas', may refer to the transept, although this seems quite late for a friary with such a long tradition of high-status burial. He was also credited with building 'the stone house that stands over the river annexed to the said west pinnacle of the said abbey, called John French's chamber'.[16] This implies a private chamber at the friary of a type noted by Donatus Mooney, who, commenting on the 'Earl's court' at the Franciscan friary of Clonmel in the early seventeenth century, noted

> for it was customary among the Irish nobles to erect edifices of this sort as places of retreat, within the bounds of monasteries of which they were the founders, and hand them over to the friars, that they might be always kept in the readiness for their reception.[17]

The friary was a favoured place of burial for the populace of Galway both before and after the suppression. Following the grant of all three friaries as cemeteries to the wardens of St Nicholas' in 1551, the role of the friary as necropolis for some of the most influential families in the town apparently continued as normal, even down to the hierarchical charges for burial places; burial in the 'chancel before any of the altars' costing £1 6s., in the body of the abbey 6s. 8d. or 'without the precinct' 2s. 8½d.[18] This not only helped to ensure the preservation of the friary church but, even after its conversion to a county court house in 1610, led to the construction of semi-private mortuary chapels whenever the tenacious friars managed to regain even the weakest of footholds at the site. Thus, in 1611 Valentine Blake FitzWalter FitzThomas, then mayor of Galway, erected a family mortuary chapel on the south side of the chancel.[19] This in spite of, as Donatus Mooney put it, 'the court [being] held in the very choir of the Franciscan church, and the judges sit[ting] on the high altar itself'.[20] In 1642, following the reclamation of Galway by the confederates, Richard Martin, of Dungorie, who was mayor of the town that year, contributed £800 towards the construction of chapels here, and at St Nicholas'.[21] These are possibly represented on the pictorial map, one built at the west end of the church, its west wall contiguous with the main west façade, another abutting the north wall of the chancel. Even as late as 1689, when the friary buildings briefly returned to the hands of the friars, Richard Martin bequeathed funds for the erection of a chapel and monument in the friary.[22]

The erection of chapels abutting original friary buildings was a common occurrence throughout the seventeenth century, with Roman Catholic families keen to maintain familial burial rights even

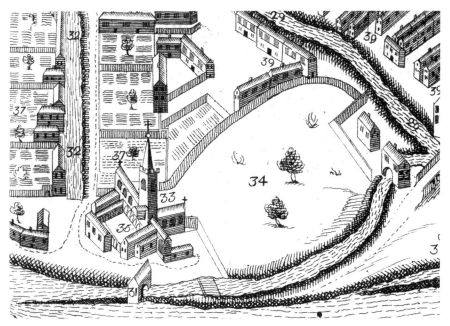

2. Galway Franciscan friary, mid-seventeenth century. Trinity College Dublin, reproduced by kind permission of the Board

after the communities of friars and the buildings where they had once commemorated the dead were gone, or much diminished. Often, as in pre-Reform chantries, these chapels were dominated by imposing monuments that contained remarkably explicit references to their patrons' faith.

A single panel and heraldic plaque survive from one such monument at the Franciscan friary. Sir Peter French died in 1631 and was commemorated by his widow, Mary Browne, by a large tomb, carved at a cost of £500 and 'gilded with gold'.[23] Presumably located in the French family chapel, erected some one hundred years earlier, the monument was short lived, being used in part to make new chimney pieces for the governor Peter Stubbers and the remainder sold at considerable expense in England.[24] These were probably classical elements such as obelisks, columns and pediments, popular in tomb design at the time. The lower parts of this monument were 'dug up' at the orders of friar Anthony Carroll and placed in the wall of the sacristy, formerly the chapel erected by Valentine Blake in the

eighteenth century and are now set into the wall of the Franciscan
friary car park.[25] The tomb's iconography, discussed below, bears
testament to the endurance of certain saints' cults in Galway.

The Dominican priory of St-Mary-on-the-Hill at the Claddagh in
Galway owed its origins to the patronage of the Lynch family who
were notable benefactors of their *confrères* in Athenry. In 1488, Pope
Innocent VIII permitted the friars to take possession of a disused
chapel, formerly the property of the Premonstratensian canons of
Tuam. Established in 1235, it had, by this time, fallen into ruin.

Construction of the new Dominican friary probably started
shortly after the grant of the site to the order at Athenry in 1488.[26]
The Lynches, already generous benefactors to the order at Athenry,
were the primary benefactors; James Lynch FitzStephen (d. 1493)
built the choir at his own expense, while Dominic *Dubh* Lynch left
£6 towards 'works to the chapel of Mary-on-the-Hill'.[27]

In 1642, Lord Forbes had established a battery there, desecrating
and burning the graves.[28] With the impending threat of attack from
Cromwellian forces in 1651, it was decided that the site made the
town too vulnerable to attack and the church was demolished. This
was done with the permission of the friars, on the understanding that
in more peaceful times the friary might be rebuilt. For this reason,
there survives a rare, measured description of the building on the eve
of its destruction.[29] Although the church was already gone by the
time the pictorial map was made, the 1651 description demonstrates
that its depiction is probably quite accurate (fig. 3).

The choir was 21.3m x 6.7m (70 x 22 feet), the nave shorter at
19.5m (64 feet). The nave was close to the same size as at Athenry,
but the choir at Galway was almost 6m longer, suggesting high hopes
for the establishment of a large community of friars and ample burial
space for patrons. The division between the two was marked by a bell
tower. The nave had a north aisle, of similar width to the nave itself,
separated from it by a four-bay arcade, and a north transept chapel
5.8m x 4.9m (19 x 16 feet). This was just over half the height of the
nave and choir – at just 3.7m (12 feet) in contrast to the 7m (23 feet) of

3. Galway Dominican friary, mid-seventeenth century. Trinity College Dublin, reproduced by kind permission of the Board

the rest of the church. It likely contained the much-venerated image of the Virgin Mary that belonged to the friars.[30] The north aisle and transept mirrored the plan of Athenry, where they represented later additions to the original church, but there the transept was longer, and the north aisle narrower. The choir at Galway was lit by a large, five-light east window. The original position of the cloister, to the south of the choir, is confirmed by the presence of just one twin-light window in the south wall, probably lighting the altar. The north of the choir was lit by six single-light windows; reference to a second, two-light 'gable' window in the choir suggests the presence of a small side chapel. As the choir was patronized by the same Lynch patron who paid for the glazing of the windows at St Nicholas', it is reasonable to assume that the tracery at St Mary's was like that in the south aisle of the collegiate church, under construction at the same time. The nave was lit by two three-light windows in its western gables and three three-light windows 'in the bodie of the church'. These are shown on the north side in the pictorial map, suggesting that much of the south side had been blocked by the claustral buildings. Reference to the battlements and 'hued' stone being re-used for repairs at St Nicholas' following demolition suggests construction in the same fine ashlar as found at the collegiate church in the post-1486 phases of construction.

ST AUGUSTINE'S, FORTHILL

The priory of St Augustine at Galway was the last foundation established by the Austin friars in Ireland before the Reformation.[31] Different authorities give either 1500 or 1506 as the date of foundation, with recent scholarship favouring the latter date.[32] The house was established by Margaret Athy, at the request of Friar Richard Nangle, professor of theology and later vicar provincial or regional superior of the Irish Augustinian friars. Her husband, Stephen FitzDominic *Dubh* Lynch, a wealthy merchant and sometime mayor of the town, was also a major benefactor of the new foundation. On his death in 1536 he bequeathed nine properties to the community.[33] Friar Nangle accepted the royal supremacy and was appointed bishop of Clonfert by Henry VIII in 1536, although he was unable to gain possession of his see in the face of local opposition. He remained in Dublin, much valued for his learning and ability to preach in Irish, where he assisted the first reformed archbishop, George Browne, himself a former superior of the English Augustinians.[34]

Like St-Mary-on-the-Hill, St Augustine's was built at the turn of the fifteenth and sixteenth centuries by members of the extended Lynch family. The friars' residence at the site was relatively short-lived and they moved to a house in the town shortly after the suppression. In 1602 the buildings were converted into a fort by Josias Bodley (fig. 4).

Both Bodley's plan and a short description of his works survive, providing useful insight into the original form of the church. He converted the nave into a store for munitions and built a solid wall at the crossing so that the choir could be used for divine service.[35] The fort was demolished in 1643 and buildings returned to the friars and restored. However, in 1645 concerns over the security of the town led to plans for its demolition, finally executed around 1652. Like the Dominican friary, a schedule of works was drawn up by the

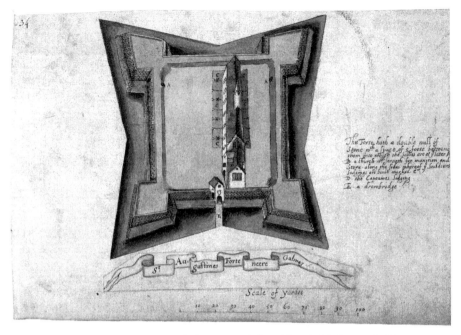

4. Josias Bodley, 'St Augustine's forte neere Galway' (1611). BL Cotton Augustus MS I.ii, fo. 34. Copyright British Library Board

corporation, on the understanding that once peacetime came they might rebuild the church at an alternative site. As with the Dominican friary, this gives an unusually accurate view of what the church was like.

The church, choir and nave combined measured 37.1m x 6.7m (121 feet 9 inches x 22 feet). It was lit by a large four-light gable window at the east (partially blocked by the later construction of a house for use of the captain of the fort) and a three-light window in the west gable. Two smaller gable windows of two lights are noted in the side walls, together with six single-light windows. The distribution of these is unclear, so unhelpful in ascertaining where, if at all, the original conventual buildings may have been located. Two 'great gates' or ceremonial doorways are noted, together with four smaller doors. The roof was still intact, as was the steeple, which rose to a height of 18.3m (60 feet). The whole was made from 'hewd' stone.[36]

The description compares well to Bodley's drawing of the church, showing a relatively long, narrow building with steeple and little sign

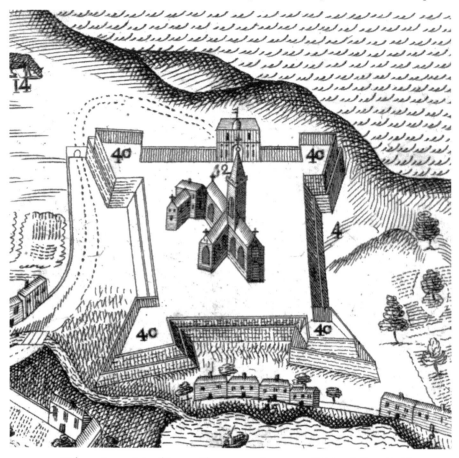

5. Galway Augustinian friary, mid-seventeenth century. Trinity College Dublin, reproduced by kind permission of the Board

of any conventual buildings. The two 'gates' suggest the presence of a west and south doorway, as, for example, at the Augustinian friary in Adare. Four smaller doors possibly relate to access to the then vanished conventual buildings, or may have been later additions, giving access to the divided 'church' and 'store' spaces of the fort. The representation on the pictorial map diverges from Bodley's map both in the orientation of the church, but also, significantly, in showing a north transept (fig. 5). Walsh suggested that this might represent a late extension to the church, made by the friars when they reoccupied the site in 1643.[37] However, were this the case, it would have been included in the inventory. This suggests that the mapmaker was either alluding to a long-lost but remembered feature, or that it was simply a figment of his imagination.

A single uncertain reference survives relating to the foundation of a Carmelite friary in Galway by a member of the de Burgh family in *c*.1332. This does not seem to have lasted very long although the Carmelites did have a house in the town in the seventeenth century.[38]

ANCHORITES, VOWESSES AND HOSPITALLERS

In addition to the religious orders, the medieval church provided other forms of consecrated life for devout Christians and there is some evidence for this in medieval Galway. These included individuals living as hermits, anchoresses, vowesses, members of Third-Order groups associated with the mendicant friars and vowed brothers and sisters who provided nursing care in medieval hospitals.

Anchorites or recluses adopted an austere penitential lifestyle enclosed in small cells called anchorholds often abutting the north wall of a church or chapel. These were equipped with internal windows or squints through which the inmate could observe the liturgical celebrations within the church. Anchorites depended on alms for their support and often had proctors who begged on their behalf. Their material needs were attended to by a servant and each anchorite's cell had an external window through which food and other items were passed. It also enabled them to offer advice and counsel to those who called to the cell, and some were highly regarded as spiritual directors and intercessors. In 1420, John Óg Blake of Galway bequeathed a vat of butter and a measure of grain to 'Fergal the anchorite' in the *pro anima* section of his will.[39] The location of the anchorhold was not specified but, if it was in Galway, it was probably attached to either the church of St Nicholas or to that of the Franciscan friary. The detailed description of the Dominican priory in 1651 discussed above also contains details of a structure on the north side of the chancel that was used as a lazar house or isolation chamber for plague victims. It is possible that its original function was as an anchorhold.

The vocation of a vowess sometimes proved attractive to devout widows of high social standing across medieval Europe and Irish references indicate their presence in Dublin and Kilkenny in the fourteenth and fifteenth centuries.[40] This calling enabled them to publicly profess vows of chastity and commit themselves to a regime of prayer and good works while maintaining control of their financial affairs. They were identifiable by their sober dark clothing and a distinctive mantle and veil, which they wore in church.[41] Though not explicitly stated, the description in the Athenry register of Margaret *Ballach* Lynch, widow of Mayor Thomas Martin of Galway, as living in 'honest widowhood' for many years after the death of her husband, 'distributing her largesse to the poor for the love of God' may indicate that she was a vowess.[42]

There is a single reference to a community of 'Poor nuns of St Francis' in Galway in 1511, when Walter Lynch, twice mayor of the town, granted a house near the church of St Nicholas to his daughter, who was a member of the community. Though nothing further is known of them, this may have been a community of regular tertiaries.[43] It has been suggested that a fifteenth-century English translation of the Third-Order rule was made for a community of sisters in Ireland. If this is the case, the Galway house seems the obvious location, as some of the male members of the other houses would have been literate in Latin and, in any case, these communities would have spoken Irish.[44] Such communities were common on the Continent in the fifteenth century, with perhaps the best known being the Grey Sisters, who ran hospitals in Flanders and Burgundy. These followed the Third-Order rule but adopted constitutions appropriate to community living and their apostolate.[45] Andrea Knox has recently noted the claims of the Spanish Dominican community at Bilboa to trace its foundation to a group of Dominican sisters from Galway who established a foundation there in 1499. This suggests the existence of a contemporary Dominican nunnery in Galway but no evidence for such a foundation survives in Irish sources before the 1630s.[46]

Like elsewhere in medieval Europe, the provision of healthcare in Galway fell under the aegis of the church and was regarded as a meritorious act, one of the 'corporal works of mercy'. The earliest expression of this was a hospital or hospice of St Mary on the western bank of the mouth of the River Corrib established by the Ó hAllmhuráin (O'Halloran) family in 1235 as a dependency of the abbey of the Holy Trinity in Tuam.[47] This was a house of

Premonstratensian or Norbertine regular canons, an order first established in northern France in 1121 and introduced to Ireland as part of the programme of reform that transformed the Irish church in the twelfth century.[48] These hospices were features of Premonstratensian ministry across Europe and offered care for the sick and indigent as well as hospitality to travellers. The Galway foundation was ideally located adjacent to the crossing point on the Corrib beside the Anglo-Norman settlement, and it may also have served the spiritual needs of the residents of the Claddagh suburb. Little is otherwise known of the foundation and in the late fifteenth century its ownership was a matter of dispute between the Norbertines and the Franciscans. Eventually, in 1488, it was granted to the Dominican friars as the site for their new foundation.

The establishment of the Franciscan friary on St Stephen's Island in 1296 led Brendan Jennings to suggest that the site was originally a leper hospital, as these were often dedicated to St Stephen or St Leonard, deacon saints associated with the service of the sick.[49] In 1504, the hospital of St Nicholas for the poor inhabitants of Galway was established by Stephen Lynch and was still in existence in the mid-seventeenth century when it was depicted on the pictorial map.[50] In 1542, St Brigid's hospital on *Bothár Mór* was established initially for the care of impoverished citizens, but later for the welfare of lepers. Each Sunday a burgess of the town was appointed to send a maidservant to quest for alms on behalf of the hospital. Its endowment also included the rights to an eel weir as well as a salmon each Friday taken out of the city weir. Destroyed in 1597 by the forces of Red Hugh O'Neill, it remained in ruins until the 1640s when an attempt was made to restore it by Francis Kirwan, a Galway native and bishop of Killala.[51]

The reference to a Templar connection with the early church in Galway has been discussed above and dismissed. However, a site on south side of what is now Eyre Square is identified as 'the place where the house of the Templars formerly stood, as tradition says'.[52] This may refer to the presence of a 'frankhouse', a single property exempt from tallages and other taxes, which both the Knights Templar and the Knights Hospitaller were permitted to own in each borough in England and Ireland.[53] These often functioned as inns and provided a source of income to the orders in addition to accommodating their members when travelling.

5. Devoted people

Devotion to God and the saints was integral to the spiritual lives of the people of Galway, as it was to Christians across medieval Europe. Saints' days and liturgical commemorations punctuated the calendar and provided the framework for feasting and fasting, business and leisure, public celebration and private devotion.[1] Although relatively little religious iconography survives from Galway, the dedications of the various altars and chapels in St Nicholas' Church and references to feast days in the corporation records provide an intimate snapshot of the city's religious life. The 1631 tomb of Sir Peter French is particularly valuable for the evidence it provides of Catholic devotion in early modern Galway. All of the saints depicted were venerated in pre-Reformation settings as well and the iconography is testimony to the enduring nature of their cults (fig. 6).

A heraldic plaque shows the impaled arms of French and Browne, flanked by SS Patrick and Nicholas. Both are depicted in the vestments of a Tridentine bishop, Patrick holding a double-armed or primatial cross. Patrick, on the left, is shown crushing snakes beneath his feet, while St Nicholas is adjacent to a child climbing from a vessel – a reference to the tradition that the saint had resurrected the dismembered remains of three boys from a pickling barrel. The larger panel, which would originally have formed the base of the tomb, has two registers of figures set under arcades. In the upper register is a defaced image of the crucifixion, flanked by the two Marys, and eight of the twelve apostles. Beneath them are the remaining four apostles, flanked on the left by Franciscan saints, SS Clare, Anthony of Padua and on the right St Francis, St Michael and St Dominic.

Devotion to the Godhead is indicated by the presence of a Trinity chapel in St Nicholas' as well as in the survival of at least three, and possibly four, early modern depictions of the Blessed Trinity from the town. On a stone from the Franciscan friary, Christ is depicted

6. Panel from the tomb of Peter French, Galway. Edwin Rae, © TRIARC, Irish Art Research Centre

with a cross while God the Father wears a cope and a papal tiara. The Holy Spirit is depicted in the form of a dove. The same configuration occurs in the depiction from St Nicholas' Church now preserved in Galway Cathedral.[2] Devotion to the person of Christ is evident in the presence of a Jesus chapel in St Nicholas', which was probably the focus for Christocentric devotions like the 'Jesus Mass' or the 'Mass of the Five Wounds'. These were popular in England and elsewhere in Ireland, particularly in churches whose choral foundations possessed the musical resources to sing the repertoire associated with the cult.[3] The great crucifix on the rood lofts of the town's churches would also have been the focus of intense devotion and a reminder of Christ's passion, death and resurrection, particularly during the dramatic ceremonies of Holy Week.

The most striking example of communal devotion to Christ was the annual celebration of the feast of *Corpus Christi*. With the extension of the feast to the universal church by Pope Urban IV in 1264 eucharistic devotions, processions and guilds became defining features of late medieval towns and cities. This emphasis on the eucharist highlighted the community's social cohesion as members of the mystical body of Christ. In Drogheda in 1412, a *Corpus Christi* sermon on this very point by a Dominican friar served to end a feud between two factions in the town and led to its incorporation as a united borough.[4] *Corpus Christi* processions also legitimized social and civic hierarchy as reflected by the order of precedence of the participating social groups. Detailed instructions for the *Corpus Christi* procession in Dublin survive from the late fifteenth century, which indicate the roles that the various merchants' guilds and social groups undertook.[5] In both Dublin and York, responsibility for organizing the procession fell to the cities' merchants' guilds, which were dedicated to *Corpus Christi*. Although no reference for such a guild survives in any Galway source, it is likely that the Blessed Sacrament chapel in St Nicholas' functioned as chapel for some high-status group, possibly a *Corpus Christi* guild. The representation of seven *Corpus Christi* street altars on the pictorial map indicates that the city hosted an extensive eucharistic procession in the mid-seventeenth century, the organization of which would presumably have fallen to city's governing elite.[6]

The cult of the Virgin Mary was the most widespread devotion in the medieval church and was found in various guises in pre-Reformation Galway. The city's Dominican priory, St-Mary-on-the-Hill, preserved a dedication that dated back to its origins as the chapel of the Premonstratensian hospice. St Nicholas' Church had two chapels dedicated to her, with one having its own dedicated priest and clerk.[7] The celebration of a daily 'Mary Mass' in St Nicholas' has already been noted and an image of the Virgin occurs on the French tomb. As noted above, the Dominican priory also possessed a celebrated image of St Mary and indulgences were granted to those who visited their church on Marian feast days.

Closely associated with the cult of the Virgin Mary was that of St Anne. Venerated as the mother of Mary and grandmother of Jesus, she was popular among older matrons and women hoping to conceive. In addition, she provided protection against plague and pestilence, saved those in peril at sea, guarded against sudden death and dying, cured melancholia, and protected those among enemies or thieves.[8] Her cult in Ireland is evident from the early thirteenth century, when, in 1212, the Knights Hospitallers had dedicated a chapel to St Anne in Cork. In Dublin, her feast was celebrated as a holiday of obligation from

1351, after a decision made by the Provincial Council at Dublin.[9] The St Anne's guild in Dublin's St Audoen's church was one of the wealthiest in the city and possessed an extensive property portfolio that it used to finance its liturgical and charitable activities.[10]

The cult of St Michael and the angels enjoyed great popularity in medieval Ireland as it did throughout Europe.[11] Venerated as the prince of the heavenly host who did battle against the forces of evil, he also presided at the Last Judgment. He was frequently shown holding a balance in which the soul and its deeds were measured and is depicted in this guise on the tomb of Sir Peter French. This eschatological role is likewise evident in the 1468 preamble to the will of John FitzHenry Blake, who entrusted his soul to St Michael, 'the wonderful messenger of prowess, the provost of paradise, to whom the Most High had assigned the reception and custody of holy souls'.[12] The guardian angels also engaged in spiritual combat with demons at the deathbeds of Christians and the presence of a chapel of St Michael and the angels is indicative of devotion to them in medieval Galway.

Devotion to the apostles is evident from their depiction on the side panels of Sir Peter French's tomb where they appear as paired couples bearing their characteristic emblems. This was a common way of representing them and is found in a number of other settings in Ireland, most notably at Cashel Cathedral, Waterford Cathedral and Kilcooly Abbey. It recalled the belief that each apostle had contributed a phrase to the 'Apostles Creed', one of the basic prayers that all Christians were expected to know.[13] Devotion to the Apostle James was particularly widespread on account of the popularity of his shrine at Santiago de Compostela as a pilgrimage destination. In 1508, Dominic *Dubh* Lynch left instructions to his son, Stephen, that an altar to the saint be erected in St Nicholas' Church. As Bernadette Cunningham notes, there were three churches or chapels and two holy wells dedicated to St James in the vicinity of Galway, an indication of the popularity of his cult.[14] The town was also an embarkation point for pilgrims to Compostela and Margaret Athy, wife of Mayor Stephen Lynch fitz Dominick and co-founder of the Augustinian priory, undertook the pilgrimage there sometime after 1508–9.[15]

The presence of four mendicant communities in Galway provided channels for other distinctive forms of devotion. The French tomb

contains depictions of the Franciscan saints Anthony of Padua,
Clare of Assisi and Francis of Assisi along with St Dominic, founder
of the Dominican order.[16] Another free-standing stone statue of a
Franciscan saint survives.[17] No devotional material remains from the
Augustinian priory at Forthill, but the dedication of a nearby holy
well to St Augustine provides evidence for his cult.[18] The strong
connection of the Lynch family with the Dominican order is evident
in the Christian names of the brothers Dominic and Peter Lynch
who presumably were christened in honour of St Dominic and of
the order's first martyr, Peter of Verona (d. 1252). Both these cults
were actively promoted by the Dominicans and in 1254 the order's
general chapter meeting in Budapest decreed that every Dominican
church should have images of both saints. In Ireland, the cult of St
Peter Martyr was actively promoted by the friars at Lorrha, Co.
Tipperary.[19]

Increasingly, from the thirteenth century onwards, saints' power
became detached from their relics and attached to their images,
which became the focus of devotion in innumerable parish churches
and chapels across Europe. A common cast of saints emerged, each
charged with responsibility for some aspect of human affairs. As
intercessors before God they became kind neighbours and allies to
their human clients. Of these a group known as the Fourteen Holy
Helpers became particularly popular. These included St Catherine
of Alexandria, to whom a guild chapel was dedicated in St Nicholas'
Church. She held numerous patronages and was invoked by civic
leaders, maidens, students and philosophers.[20] The 'Holy Helpers'
also included figures like St Margaret of Antioch, invoked by women
in labour; St Christopher, the patron saint of travellers; St Sebastian,
invoked for protection at times of plague, and St Apollonia, the
patroness of those suffering from toothache. Evidence for their cults
occurs elsewhere in Ireland and they would also have been venerated
in medieval Galway.

Devotion to Irish saints is evident in the dedication of a chapel
to St Patrick in St Nicholas' Church along with his depiction on the
French tomb. As already noted, the collegiate church also contained
an altar to St Bridget and the leper hospital dedicated to her was
established *c*.1542 at *Bothár Mór*. Whereas these dedications were
most likely to St Bridget of Kildare, Ireland's secondary patron, it

is possible, given Galway's international trading connections, that the saint commemorated was St Bridget of Sweden (d. 1373), whose mystical text the *Fifteen Ooes* is found in Middle English translation in a devotional manuscript produced in Dublin in the mid-fifteenth century.[21] More local devotion is evident in the dedication of a well to St Brendan, the patron saint of Annaghdown, near the de Burgh castle.[22]

BIRTHS, DEATHS AND MARRIAGES

In addition to the moral oversight that the corporation exercised over the town's clergy, the city fathers also legislated for the sexual mores of the citizens. An ordinance of 1505 forbade anyone from maintaining a brothel or housing prostitutes in the town on pain of a fine of 6s. 6d.[23] In 1519, it was enacted that any man who impregnated a merchant's or freeman's daughter had to either to marry her himself or make sufficient provision for her to marry another.[24] No evidence survives for how marriages were conducted in Galway but doubtless the church struggled to enforce its norms in the face of less formal arrangements.[25] Where arrangements are recorded they relate to elite couples for whom the issue of the legitimacy of offspring and succession rights were paramount. In 1468, an agreement was made between John Blake and Peter Lynch of Galway whereby the latter agreed to marry the former's daughter, Evelyn Blake. A dowry of sixty marks was agreed. However, as both parties were related within the forbidden degrees of consanguinity, a papal dispensation had to be procured, the cost of which was be born jointly by the bride's father and her betrothed. In the interim, Lynch swore to regard as legitimate any offspring borne before the dispensation was received and the marriage solemnized.[26] In 1472, Pope Sixtus IV granted a similar dispensation to Walter Blake and Juliana Lynch and legitimated their offspring.[27]

The birth of a child was a cause for celebration but the lavish celebratory banquets hosted by some of the town's mothers were forbidden by decree of the corporation in 1536. Women who did not comply risked a fine of twenty shillings while those who went seeking refreshment uninvited risked a forfeit of 6s. 6d.[28]

No such parsimony was evident in making provision for the soul as the small number of wills that survive from Galway demonstrate. In addition to the chantries, mausoleums and dynastic tombs discussed above, the town's elite made generous provision for their post-mortem welfare. John Óg Blake (d. 1420) left five marks to the Franciscans in Galway where he was buried in the Blake's ancestral tomb and where seven of the community received personal bequests. He likewise made offerings to the church of St Nicholas for forgotten tithes and for the maintenance fund of the chapel of St Anne. His bequest to the 'house of the poor' included two measures of corn and one of peas. Other beneficiaries included the secular clergy and all the mendicant houses in Connacht.[29] Ongoing intercession included endowing commemorations at which the Office for the Dead (the *Dirige* or 'dirge') was sung and an anniversary Mass celebrated. The funds for these often came from rents accruing from tenements and properties and were occasionally contested by later occupants. In 1596, the warden and vicars of the college had to appeal to the mayor and corporation to enforce payment of sums outstanding for five endowed commemorations.[30]

Burial in the habit of a friar would doubtless have been sought by their devotees in Galway but no record of this survives. A popular practice was to secure a letter of confraternity from a mendicant house whereby benefactors were granted a share in the suffrages, prayers and spiritual exercises of the community. In 1521, Friar David O'Hyrella, the Franciscan minister provincial, admitted Alexander Lynch fitzJohn and his wife Anastacia Lynch to confraternity with the order.[31]

THE RITUAL YEAR

The liturgical calendar gave shape to much of the civic life of medieval Galway as it did to communities across Europe. Mayors of Galway and other officials were elected to office on the feast of St Michael (29 September) and their election was the occasion of civic celebrations and feasting. In 1517, the corporation decreed that no hangers-on should follow the new mayor to his house in expectation of hospitality without receiving an invitation.[32] Within a month of Michaelmas, the mayor was obliged to summon an assembly of freemen for the purpose of auditing accounts and admitting freemen and similar gatherings were held at Christmas, Easter and Midsummer.[33] In 1584, in what was probably a reassertion of an ancient custom, the corporation decreed that the masons and carpenters working on civic works were to be entertained at the mayor's expense at the Midsummer and Michaelmas feasts.[34]

Certain feast days were observed as holidays on which no physical labour was undertaken. In 1526, the corporation decreed that those engaging the services of carpenters and masons were not obliged to feed them on these days unless they were employed for a fixed term. On St Catherine's Day (25 November) 1507, the mayor Arthur Lynch and the bailiffs William Joyce and Anthony Lynch were drowned when they fell from the town's western bridge into the Corrib.[35] Although not stated, it is possible that they were performing a civic inspection similar to the 'riding of the franchises' regularly undertaken by the mayors of Dublin to perambulate the city's boundaries and inspect its features.[36] In Galway, one such demarcating landmark, *Cloch an Loinsigh* 'Lynch's rock', still survives in Renmore.[37]

In addition to the annual *Corpus Christi* procession described above, Galway's citizens would have participated in the various Rogation processions in spring and early summer when the clergy took to the streets singing litanies and reciting prayers invoking God's blessing on crops and beseeching deliverance from pestilence and attack.[38] It is possible that the numerous crosses depicted on the pictorial map indicate stopping points or 'stations' on this processional way.[39] These events also served to fix parochial landmarks and boundaries in the collective memory of the parishioners.

The highlights of the year were the festivities at Christmas and Easter.[40] In addition to the religious celebrations, the assemblies of freemen also added colour to civic life. These were also occasions on which hospitality was expected and extended, sometimes to excess. In 1518, the corporation forbade householders from entertaining members of the Burke, MacWilliam and Ó Ceallaigh families without prior permission. Likewise, in 1544, it listed priests, doctors and clerks at the head of a list of professions banned from importuning householders for 'offerings or other dainties' on the feast days themselves or on the twelve days following them.[41]

The celebrations at May Day were a three-day event at which the youth of the town competed at various sports and athletic contests including 'tilting at the ring' which is depicted on the pictorial map.[42] This involved a rider attempting to insert a lance into a metal ring or hoop while riding at full tilt. On the third day of the games, the young men of the town rode out to Blake's Hill near Barna on the outskirts of the town for further sporting and feasting.[43] St John's or Midsummer's Eve was another occasion of celebration on which a mayoral banquet took place.[44] It is likely that the festivities included merrymaking around bonfires as was customary elsewhere in Ireland.[45]

POSTSCRIPT: THE LYNCH FAMILY AS PATRONS

Over a period of about twenty years, between c.1486 and 1506, the physical Christian landscape of Galway was altered radically. Almost simultaneously, the city gained a much-enlarged collegiate church, two new religious houses of significant scale, a hospital, a nunnery and a chapel dedicated to St James. These developments were thanks in large measure to one extremely powerful family: the Lynches.

Investment in the civic fabric by the family was not a new phenomenon. Extracts pertaining to the Lynch family from a list of 'public and spiritual works' undertaken by the people of Galway kept by the wardens of St Nicholas' in the mid-seventeenth century provide a particularly valuable insight into their patronage.[46] Works in the early fourteenth century include construction of the 'great gate' by Nicholas Lynch in 1312;[47] and sponsorship of the new nave of St Nicholas', mentioned above. These would have had a substantial visual impact on Galway town at the time, the great gate simultaneously controlling entry to the town and symbolizing its burgeoning power, the church providing arguably the largest civic space in the town.

The works over the turn of the fifteenth and sixteenth centuries were equally an expression of civic power, prestige and piety. Large mendicant houses with steeples, located at prominent locations, created a complex skyline to greet merchants arriving by sea. Together with their pious functions, the towers of these new structures (and probably an enlarged tower on St Nicholas') provided navigational aid and, as has been shown, a safe place to store goods. In addition, sections of the town walls were extended, including the 'shoemaker's tower' initiated under the mayoralty of James Lynch FitzMartin.[48] With the possible exception of Dublin at the turn of the twelfth and thirteenth centuries, no Irish town had ever seen construction on a similar scale over such a relatively short period of time.

In addition to the amount of construction, unlike most large stone buildings encountered by visitors to Irish towns, the architectural additions to Galway at this time had a refinement more common to the civic architecture of the overseas ports, leading many later visitors to the town to evoke comparisons with Spain. The Lynch buildings were constructed from smooth limestone ashlar with battlemented parapets. Native Irish limestone is exceptionally hard, so making it costly and time-consuming to cut into blocks. As a result, its use for walling in Ireland was rare. This, together with rich sculptural detailing, suggest a sizeable community of specialist masons working in Galway at the time. Incorporation of heraldry and merchants' marks in the fabric ensured that the funders of these works would not easily be forgotten.

At almost exactly the same time as the extension to St Nicholas' and construction of the Augustinian and Dominican friaries, a new college building was constructed to the west of the church, together with a grand new urban dwelling.

The college building was initiated by John Lynch FitzEdmond, who mas mayor in 1494–5; John Lynch FitzJohn and Dominic *Dubh* Lynch also bequeathed money to it in 1496 and 1508 respectively.[49] The buildings were demolished in the early nineteenth century. However, writing in the latter part of the seventeenth century, Fr John Lynch noted that the arms of Dominic *Dubh* were positioned over the college gate. The only remnant that survives is the reader's desk that now occupies the entrance of the Blessed sacrament chapel at St Nicholas'. Its fine barley twist column suggests a quality of masonry comparable to that of the surviving works of the period.

Conspicuously located on the corner of what is now Shop Street and Abbeygate Street Upper, the Lynches invested in a new urban residence at the same time as their ecclesiastical ventures. Also built of neat ashlar, the large tower house is distinguished by the quantity and quality of stone sculpture that adorns the façade.[50]

This includes the arms of the Lynch family together with those of Henry VII and of the FitzGeralds of Kildare. The combination of these arms suggests a date around 1500; Henry's reign extended from 1485 to 1509, Gerald FitzGerald was lord deputy when the forces of Ulick Burke were defeated at the battle of Knockdoe in 1504. The sculptural embellishment is predominantly secular, but includes two inscriptions, now positioned beneath the Lynch and Kildare heraldry respectively: 'After the darkness I hope for light' (Job 17:2) and 'He hath deposed the mighty from their seat, and he hath exalted the humble' (Luke 1:52).[51] The tall roofline of the castle, originally battlemented and with projecting gargoyle waterspouts, provided a strong visual link with the contemporary south aisle of St Nicholas' nearby. It was perhaps no accident that one nineteenth-century visitor to Galway noted the church was 'something between a church and a castle, as if it should be served by Templars with sword and helmet, in place of mitre and crozier'.[52]

While sufficient remnants and descriptions of the Lynch's architectural patronage remain to give an impression of its character, much less can be recovered of their contribution to their interiors. Earlier in the fifteenth century, Lynch benefactions to the Dominican friary at Athenry were recorded in the friary *Register*. These included repairs to the figure of the rood and statue of St Dominic, the latter presumably dominating the altar in front of which the Lynches had a family vault.[53] During the mid-fifteenth century, one member of the family in particular was singled out for his munificence to the friars. Edmund Lynch (d. 1462), sometime sovereign of Galway, in 1434 and 1443 gave gifts that included new tracery and glass for windows in the north part of the nave, two sets of cloth-of-gold vestments and a missal and pontifical. The *Register* also records his erection of a family tomb in St Nicholas'.[54] As noted above, this may have been the wall tomb with flamboyant tracery and figure of Christ Judging. If this is the case, it was to set the fashion for a number of similar tombs created across Connacht in the late fifteenth and early sixteenth centuries.

Together with sculpted heraldry and imagery in wall paintings and stained glass, the refurbishment or foundation of churches was often commemorated by the donation of altar plate.[55] For example, an altar cross commissioned for Lislaughtin Friary in Kerry by Cornelius O'Connor in 1479 commemorated his father's foundation of the friary itself.[56] The base of a 1494 chalice, most likely the product of a Galway goldsmith's workshop, commemorated the donors, Thomas de Burgh and Grainne O'Malley, on the upper side of the base. This ensured their remembrance at the very moment of the elevation of the vessel.[57]

It is more likely than not that the elevation of St Nicholas' Church to collegiate status and foundation of the two new friaries were commemorated in a similar way. Dominic *Dubh*'s will includes an 8oz silver cup to be bequeathed to the college in Galway.[58] An inventory of some of St Nicholas' altar plate is provided in 1546, when it was put in pledge with another member of the extended Lynch family, James Lynch FitzRichard. The 'juelles of ye chyrche' were recorded at that time as comprising a 'grete cross of shylver', four silver candlesticks (two bracket, two freestanding), a pyx for the sacrament, and four silver chalices.[59] Although none of these can be definitively linked to the family, one of two pyxes from the church pawned by a warden in 1583 is described as being that donated by Margaret Athy, wife of Stephen Lynch.[60]

The nature and quantity of plate, vestments, service books and other devotional paraphernalia donated by the Lynches will probably never be known, but what is certain is that it will have been of high quality, and at least some of foreign manufacture.

The combined wealth and worldliness of the Lynch family and the extended oligarchy of late medieval Galway created a town like no other in Ireland. Its unique character was attributed by later visitors to the town to its extensive trade links with the Continent. However, as noted by one nineteenth-century commentator, it was 'the extreme Roman Catholic or rather monastic character of the town, with its accompaniments of conventual chapels, conventual cemeteries and conventual archways, [that] seems really to have been the grand feature […]'.[61]

Notes

ABBREVIATIONS

AC	*Annála Connacht: the annals of Connacht, 1224–1254*, ed. A.M. Freeman (Dublin, 1944)
AD	Anno Domini
AFM	*Annála ríoghachta Éireann: Annals of the kingdom of Ireland by the Four Masters from the earliest period to the year 1616*, ed. and trans. John O'Donovan, 7 vols (Dublin, 1851; repr. New York, 1966)
ALC	*Annals of Loch Cé: a chronicle of Irish affairs, 1014–1590*, ed. W.M. Hennessy, 2 vols (London, 1871; repr. Dublin, 1939)
BL	British Library
Cal. Carew MSS	*Calendar of the Carew manuscripts preserved in the archiepiscopal library at Lambeth, 1515–74* [etc.], ed. J.S. Brewer and W. Bullen, 6 vols (London, 1860–73)
CDI	*Calendar of documents relating to Ireland, 1171–1251* [etc.], ed. H.S. Sweetman, 5 vols (London, 1875–86) [vol. 1] 1171–1251; [vol. 2] 1252–84; [vol. 3] 1285–92; [vol. 4] 1293–1301; [vol. 5], 1302–7
CLAJ	*County Louth Archaeological and Historical Journal*
col./cols	column/columns
CPR	*Calendar of entries in the papal registers relating to Britain and Ireland: papal letters*, ed. W.H. Bliss et al.
ed./eds	editor/editors
fo./fos	folio/folios
JGAHS	*Journal of the Galway Archaeological and Historical Society*
JRSAI	*Journal of the Royal Society of Antiquaries of Ireland*
MS/S	manuscript/s
n.d.	no date
NLI	National Library of Ireland
pers. comm.	personal communication
PRIA	*Proceedings of the Royal Irish Academy*
P.R.I. rep. D.K.	*Public Record Office, Ireland, report of the deputy keeper*, I [etc.]
s.a.	*sub anno* (under the year)
TCD	Trinity College Dublin

INTRODUCTION

1   Paul Walsh, *Renaissance Galway: delineating the seventeenth-century city* (Dublin, 2019).

2   J.T. Gilbert, 'Archives of the town of Galway' in *Historical Manuscripts Commission tenth report* (London, 1885), appendix, pt v, pp 380–520.

3   Some of this material was published in Roderic O'Flaherty, *A chorographical description of west or h-Iar Connaught:* *written AD1684*, ed. James Hardiman (Dublin, 1846). For the subsequent fate of these documents, see Edward McLysaght and H.F. Berry, 'Documents relating to the wardenship of Galway', *Analecta Hibernica*, 14 (1944), pp 1–3, 5, 7–141, 143–87, 189–250; Jan Power, 'Archives report: Galway diocesan archives', *Archivium Hibernicum*, 46 (1991/2), pp 135–8.

1. ESTABLISHING THE CHURCH

1 Jacinta Prunty and Paul Walsh, *Irish Historic Towns Atlas, no. 28: Galway/ Gaillimh* (Dublin, 2016), p. 1.

2 *AFM, s.a.* 1124.

3 *AFM; ALC; AC; Pipe roll, 51 Henry III,* quoted in James Hardiman, *History of the town and county of Galway* (Dublin, 1820), p. 49n.

4 Frank Coyne, Aegis Archaeology, pers. comm. 16 Feb. 2022.

5 For what follows, see Fergal Grannell, 'Galway' in R. Aubert (ed.), *Dictionnaire d'histoire et de géographie ecclésiastique,* 31 vols (Paris, 1981), xix, cols 925–54 at cols 934–6.

6 Hubert Thomas Knox, *Notes on the early history of the dioceses of Tuam, Killala and Achonry* (Dublin, 1904), p. 148.

7 Hardiman, *History,* pp 3n, 37n.

8 *Calendar of documents relating to Ireland,* ed. H.S. Sweetman, 5 vols (London, 1875–86), v, 1302–7, pp 226, 235.

9 O'Flaherty, *Chorographical description,* p. 35.

10 Hardiman, *History,* p. 234.

11 John Fleetwood Berry, *The story of St Nicholas' Collegiate Church, Galway* (Galway, 1912), p. 11; Harold G. Leask, 'The Collegiate Church of St Nicholas, Galway', *JGAHS,* 17:1–2 (1936), pp 2–23 at p. 5.

12 Aubrey Gwynn and R.N. Hadcock, *Medieval religious houses: Ireland* (Dublin, 1970), pp 327–31. For the military orders in medieval Ireland, see the contributions to Martin Browne and Colmán Ó Clabaigh (eds), *Soldiers of Christ: the Knights Hospitaller and Knights Templar in medieval Ireland* (Dublin, 2016).

13 Catherine E. Hundley, 'Shared space: Templars, Hospitallers and the English parish church' in Meg Bernstein (ed.), *Towards an art history of the English parish church, 1200–1399* (London, 2021), pp 94–113 at pp 94–5.

14 Paul Walsh, 'The topography of the town of Galway in the medieval and early modern period' in Gerard Moran and Raymond Gillespie (eds), *Galway history and society* (Dublin, 1996), pp 27–96 at pp 56, 91n.

15 Hardiman, *History,* p. 274.

16 R.A.S. Macalister, 'The Dominican church at Athenry', *JRSAI,* 3:3 (1913),

pp 197–222 at p. 212, pl. VII nos 3, 5. No explanation is given for the implausibly late dates assigned to these slabs by Macalister.

17 Eoin C. Bairéad, 'Nicholas and Dublin' in Mary Davis, Una McConville and Gabriel Cooney (eds), *A grand gallimaufrey: collected in honour of Nick Maxwell* (Dublin, 2010), pp 152–4 at p. 152; Roger Stalley, 'The architecture of the cathedral and priory buildings' in Kenneth Milne (ed.), *Christ Church Cathedral: a history* (Dublin, 2000), p. 106.

18 R. Miller, 'The early medieval seaman and the church: contacts ashore', *The Mariner's Mirror: International Quarterly Journal of the Society for Nautical Research,* 89:2 (2003), pp 132–50 at pp 138–41.

19 Will of John Óg Blake, published in O'Flaherty, *Chorographical description,* p. 200.

20 Miriam Clyne, 'The founders and patrons of Premonstratensian houses in Ireland' in Janet Burton and Karen Stöber (eds), *The regular canons in the medieval British Isles* (Turnhout, 2011), pp 145–72 at pp 170–1.

2. GOD AND MAMMON: POLITICS AND THE PARISH

1 *P.R.I. rep. D.K.* 36, pp 47–8.

2 John Bradley, *Irish Historic Towns Atlas, no. 10: Kilkenny* (Dublin, 2000), p. 3; Cóilín Ó Drisceoil, 'Yet nothin is more certaine then death, nor more uncertaine, than the houre thereof': excavations in the chantry chapels of St Mary's Church, Kilkenny' in Christiaan Corlett and Michael Potterton (eds), *The town in medieval Ireland in the light of recent archaeological excavations* (Dublin, 2020), pp 161–84 at pp 164–5.

3 Philip H. Hore, *History of the town and county of Wexford* (London, 1900), i, p. 85; Jill Unkel, 'An enduring monument [St Mary's New Ross]', *Irish Arts Review,* 22:3 (autumn 2002), pp 100–3.

4 Philip Robinson, *Irish Historic Towns Atlas, no. 2: Carrickfergus* (Dublin, 1986), pp 2, 10; Ruairí Ó Baoill, *St Nicholas' Church, Carrickfergus, Co. Antrim. Archaeology Ireland* Heritage Guide no. 43 (Dublin, 2009).

5 Tadhg O'Keeffe, *Medieval Irish buildings, 1100–1600* (Dublin, 2015), pp 127–39; Rachel Moss, 'Irish parish churches: 1350–1550' in Paul Barnwell (ed.), *Places of worship in the British Isles, 1350–1550* (Donington, 2019), pp 174–90.

6 David Kelly, John Mulcahy and Clodagh Tait, 'St Mary's, Youghal, Co. Cork', *Irish Arts Review*, 20:1 (spring 2003), pp 114–21; Jenifer Ní Ghrádaigh, 'Fragments of a twelfth-century doorway at the church of St Multose, Kinsale?', *JRSAI*, 133 (2003), pp 68–77; J.L. Darling, *St Multose Church, Kinsale: an account historical and descriptive* (Cork, 1895).

7 John Bradley, 'The topography and layout of medieval Drogheda', *CLAJ*, 19 (1978), pp 98–137 at 114–15; H.G. Tempest, *Notes on the parish church of St Nicholas, Dundalk* (Dundalk, 1955); Oliver Davis, 'Old churches in County Louth', *CLAJ*, 10:1 (1941), pp 5–23 at pp 15–19.

8 *Calendar of Justiciary Rolls, or Proceedings in the Court of the Justiciar of Ireland, preserved in the Public Record Office of Ireland*, ed. J. Mills, H. Wood, A.E. Langman and M.C. Griffith, 3 vols (Dublin, 1905–14), iii, p. 227. This tradition appears to have continued into the early modern period, with a similar account of the attempted theft of wheat from a large bin, kept 'under the protection of the cross', recorded in the by then Anglican parish church of Holycross, Co. Tipperary, in 1611: Malachy Hartry, *Triumphalia chronologica Monasterii Sanctae Crucis in Hibernia*, ed. and trans. Denis Murphy (Dublin, 1891), pp 128–31.

9 Colmán Ó Clabaigh, *The friars in Ireland, 1224–1540* (Dublin, 2012), p. 114.

10 Miller, 'Early medieval seaman', pp 138–41.

11 Adrian Empey, 'The formation and development of intramural churches and communities in medieval Dublin' in John Bradley, Alan J. Fletcher and Anngret Simms (eds), *Dublin in the medieval world* (Dublin, 2009), pp 249–76 at pp 250–1.

12 Nicholas Orme, 'Church and chapel in medieval England', *Transactions of the Royal Historical Society*, 6 (1996), pp 75–102 at p. 87.

13 Bruce Campbell, 'Benchmarking medieval economic development: England, Wales, Scotland and Ireland, *c*.1290', *Economic History Review* 61:4 (2008), pp 896–948 at p. 911.

14 *CDI*, v, pp 226, 235. The taxation covered 'the church and rectory of Galway' and followed the tradition, unusual to the ecclesiastical province of Tuam, of the quadripartion of tithes, so that the priest and rector held three parts of the tithe, valued at 100s. per annum, while the bishop held the fourth, valued at 33s. 4d.: Kenneth Nicholls, 'Rectory, vicarage and parish in the western Irish dioceses', *JRSAI*, 101 (1971), pp 53–84 at p. 54.

15 Chris Chevalier, 'What was the distribution of wealth in Ireland, *c*.1300? Exploring medieval Ireland's economy via papal taxation records', *History Ireland*, 27:4 (2019), pp 18–21.

16 Jim McKeon, 'St Nicholas' parish church, Galway: structural and architectural evidence for the high medieval period', *Journal of Irish Archaeology*, 18 (2009), pp 95–113 at p. 97.

17 The chancel walls are 0.7m thick; the transept walls are 0.4m thick; the south nave wall is 0.5m thick.

18 John McErlean, 'Notes on the pictorial map of Galway: the index to the map', *JGAHS*, 4 (1905–6), pp 133–60 at p. 145.

19 Unless otherwise stated, this section summarizes Grannell, 'Galway' and Martin Coen, *The wardenship of Galway* (Galway, 1984), pp 1–14.

20 W.H. Bliss and J.A. Twemlow (eds), *Calendar of entries in the papal registers relating to Great Britain and Ireland: papal letters*, v, AD1396–1404 (London, 1904), pp 189, 254, 511.

21 The text of both Archbishop Ó Muireadhaigh and the bull of Innocent VIII are included in Hardiman, *History*, appendix, pp i–iv. A translation of the latter is given on pp iv–vi.

22 Ibid., p. iv.

23 The papal bulls licensing these unions are given in O'Flaherty, *Chorographical description*, pp 156–66.

24 O'Flaherty, *Chorographical description*, p. 167.

25 Mary D. O'Sullivan, *Old Galway* (Cambridge, 1942), pp 390–7.

26 Gilbert, 'Archives of Galway', pp 384–5.

27 M.K. Ó Murchadha, 'Music in St Nicholas' Collegiate Church, Galway, 1480–1912', *JGAHS*, 45 (1993), pp 29–43 at pp 29–30.

28 Gilbert, 'Archives of Galway', p. 398.

29 Ibid., p. 404.

30 Ibid., p. 387.

31 Ibid., pp 387, 395, 397.

32 O'Flaherty, *Chorographical description*, pp 236–40.

33 O'Flaherty, *Chorographical description*, pp 236–40; O'Sullivan, *Old Galway*, pp 393–5.

3. EXPERIENCING THE MEDIEVAL CHURCH

1 *Statutes and ordinances and acts of the parliament of Ireland: King John to Henry V*, ed. H.F. Berry (Dublin, 1907), p. 257; *Records of convocation: Ireland*, ed. G. Bray, 16–18, 3 vols (Woodbridge, 2006), xvi, p. 182.

2 Rachel Moss, 'An art-historical perspective on the Irish Historic Towns Atlas' in H.B. Clarke and Sarah Gearty, *More maps and texts: sources and the Irish Historic Towns Atlas* (Dublin, 2018), pp 220–38 at p. 227.

3 Anngret Simms, 'Interlocking spaces: the relative location of medieval parish churches, churchyards, marketplaces and town halls' in Howard B. Clarke and J.R.S. Phillips (eds), *Ireland, England and the Continent in the Middle Ages and beyond* (Dublin, 2006), pp 222–34.

4 *Liber Primus Kilkenniensis*, ed. and trans. J. Otway-Ruthven (Kilkenny, 1961), pp 13–14, 18–20.

5 *Liber Antiquissimus Civitatis Waterfordiae: The Great Parchment Book of Waterford*, ed. Niall Byrne (Dublin, 2007), pp 106–7.

6 Moss, 'An art-historical perspective', pp 223–6.

7 For the origins and a critical analysis of the source, see Paul Walsh, 'An account of the town of Galway', *JGAHS*, 44 (1992), pp 47–118.

8 Empey, 'The layperson in the parish', pp 7–48; idem, *The proctors' accounts of the parish church of St Werburgh, Dublin, 1481–1627* (Dublin, 2009), pp 14–20.

9 Leask, 'St Nicholas', pp 12–13; McKeon, 'St Nicholas', pp 105–10.

10 The new choir at Tuam Cathedral was begun in 1289, but was still incomplete in 1312, placing the date of its windows towards the end of the 1310s: *Cal. papal letters*, ii, 1305–42, p. 109; Miriam Clyne, 'Excavations at St Mary's Tuam, Co. Galway', *JGAHS*, 41 (1987–8), pp 90–103. At Athenry, new east and west windows were commissioned by William *Liath* de Burgh and his wife *c.*1320, shortly after his victory at the Battle of Athenry: A. Coleman (ed.), '*Regestum Monasterii Fratrum praedicatorum de Athenry*', *Archivium Hibernicum*, 1 (1912), pp 201–21 at p. 212.

11 For example, at St Multose, Kinsale, St Mary's, Kilmallock, St Audoen's, Dublin and Holy Trinity, Fethard.

12 McKeon, 'St Nicholas', pp 95–113.

13 O'Sullivan, *Old Galway* remains foundational. See also Coen, *The wardenship of Galway*, for a concise account of the development of the town's unique ecclesiastical administration.

14 Richard Pfaff, *The liturgy in medieval England: a history* (Cambridge, 2009); Matthew Cheung Salisbury, *The secular liturgical office in late medieval England* (Turnhout, 2015). There is no comprehensive account of the Use of Sarum in Ireland. For Dublin, see Alan J. Fletcher, 'Liturgy and music in the medieval cathedral' in John Crawford and Raymond Gillespie (eds), *St Patrick's Cathedral, Dublin: a history* (Dublin, 2009), pp 120–48; idem, 'Liturgy in the late medieval cathedral priory' in Milne, *Christ Church Cathedral*, pp 129–41; Peadar Slattery, *Social life in pre-Reformation Dublin, 1450–1540* (Dublin, 2019), pp 150–2, 162.

15 Ó Murchadha, 'Music', pp 29–30.

16 Rachel Moss, 'Doorways and doors' in Rachel Moss (ed.), *Art and architecture of Ireland: I Medieval, c.400–c.1600* (Dublin, 2014), pp 97–9.

17 Colmán Ó Clabaigh, 'Childbirth, christening and churching in medieval Ireland' in Salvador Ryan (ed.), *Birth and the Irish: a miscellany* (Dublin, 2021), pp 49–53.

18 Leask, 'St Nicholas", p. 19. These were partly removed following the later insertion of the window above.

19 Harold G. Leask, 'Rathmore Church, Co. Meath', *JRSAI*, 63 (1933), pp 153–66 at p. 154; Leask, 'St Nicholas", quoting the Lynch MS, p. 88.

20 Empey, *Proctor's accounts*, p. 67.

21 Archdeacon Gary Hastings, pers. comm., 30 Sept. 2018.

22 Francis Bond, *Fonts and font covers* (Oxford, 1908); Rachel Moss, 'Fonts' in Moss (ed.), *Art and architecture of Ireland*, I, pp 324–5.

23 Danielle O'Donovan, 'Callan and Ormond: an architectural middle nation?' in Emmett O'Byrne and Jenifer Ní Ghrádaigh (eds), *The march in the islands of the medieval west* (Leiden, 2012), pp 171–94 at pp 184–9.

24 A further two panels are now lying loose in the south transept, one is built into the wall of the Blessed Sacrament chapel and another was recently incorporated into the donations box: Jim Higgins and Susanne Heringklee, *Monuments of St Nicholas Collegiate Church, Galway: a historical, genealogical and archaeological record* (Galway, n.d.), pp 255–7.

25 For similar arrangements in medieval friaries, see Ó Clabaigh, *Friars*, pp 101–10.

26 While a number of these are independently referenced elsewhere, the coincidence of fourteen altars on a map that constantly references the number and its factor of seven requires caution: Walsh, *Renaissance Galway*, pp 6–7; McErlean, 'Notes on the pictorial map', pp 144–6.

27 Margaret Phelan, 'Irish sculpture portraying the five wounds of the Saviour' in Etienne Rynne (ed.), *Figures from the past: studies in figurative art in Christian Ireland* (Blackrock, 1987), pp 242–8.

28 The masonry on the exterior of the Peace Chapel and its window are of late sixteenth-century date.

29 Roger Stalley, 'Gothic survival in sixteenth-century Connacht' in Marion Meek (ed.), *The modern traveller to our past: festschrift in honour of Ann Hamlin* (Belfast, 2006), pp 302–14 at pp 311–12; ibid., 'The abbey and its context' in Conleth

Manning, Paul Gosling and John Waddell (eds), *New survey of Clare Island, 4: the abbey* (Dublin, 2005), pp 135–50 at pp 139–41; James Mitchell, 'The mistitled "Joyce" tomb in the Collegiate church of St Nicholas, Galway', *JGAHS*, 40 (1985/6), pp 138–9; Coleman, 'Regestum', p. 211.

30 Higgins and Heringklee, *Monuments of St Nicholas*, pp 305–7; Ó Drisceoil, 'Yet nothin', pp 168–73.

31 M.J. Blake, 'An old Lynch manuscript', *JGAHS*, 9:2 (1914–15), pedigree facing p. 91.

32 Steven G. Ellis, 'Sacred space and "true religion": the Irish Reformation and the Collegiate Church of St Nicholas, Galway' in *Entangled Religions: Interdisciplinary Journal for the Study of Religious Contact and Transfer*, 7 (2018), pp 14–45 at pp 31–7; Rachel Moss, 'Continuity and change: the material setting of public worship in the sixteenth century' in Thomas Herron and Michael Potterton (eds), *Dublin and the Pale in the Renaissance, 1494–1660* (Dublin, 2011), pp 182–206 at pp 192–206.

33 Walsh, 'An account', p. 66.

34 Stalley, 'Architecture of the cathedral', pp 104–5.

35 Blake, 'Old Lynch manuscript', pp 102–3; O'Flaherty, *Chorographical description*, p. 320.

36 McLysaght and Berry, 'The wardenship of Galway', pp 9, 11.

37 Blake, 'Old Lynch manuscript', p. 101.

38 Katherine J. Lewis, *The cult of St Katherine of Alexandria in late medieval England* (Woodbridge, 2000), p. 165.

39 O'Flaherty, *Chorographical description*, p. 200.

40 Ibid., p. 207.

41 Helen Roe, 'Illustrations of the Holy Trinity in Ireland: 13th to 17th centuries', *JRSAI*, 109 (1979), pp 101–50.

42 Leask, 'St Nicholas", pp 16–17. His argument rests solely on the masonry around the north-west window, the tracery of which bears the date 1583. However, elsewhere in the church he points out the 'making good' of masonry around later additions.

43 Charles McNeill, 'Accounts of sums realised by sales of chattels of some

suppressed Irish monasteries', *JRSAI*,
52 (1922), pp 11–37 at p. 15; Hardiman,
History, p. 239.

44 Ellis, 'Sacred space', pp 29–30.

45 Blake, 'Old Lynch manuscript',
pp 102–3; O'Flaherty, *Chorographical
description*, p. 320.

46 Walsh, 'Account', p. 61. We are grateful
to an tAth. Máirtín Ó Conaire for advice
on this point.

47 Hardiman, *History*, p. 243.

48 For a description of the earlier bells, see
*Journal of the Society for the Preservation of
Memorials to the Dead, Ireland*, 2 (1892–4),
p. 136.

49 TCD MS 667, p. 37.

50 E. FitzGerald, 'The acoustic vases and
other relics discovered in the church
of St Mary, Youghal', *Transactions
of the Kilkenny and South East Ireland
Archaeological Association*, ser. 1, 3:2 (1855),
pp 303–10.

51 Leask, 'St Nicholas", p. 6.

52 O'Sullivan, *Old Galway*, p. 450, citing
Egerton MSS no. 115, fos 73–82.

53 Rachel Moss, 'Window glass' in Moss,
Art and architecture of Ireland, 1,
pp 89–91.

54 E. Trocmé and M. Delafosse, *La commerce
rochelais de la fin du XVé siècle au début du
XVIIé siècle* (Paris, 1952), pp 66, 83n32.

4. THE ORDERED LIFE

1 On the emergence of the mendicant
movement in Ireland, see Ó Clabaigh,
Friars, pp 1–29.

2 NLI, D679; *Ormond deeds*, i, pp 240–2;
trans. pp 238–9.

3 Ó Clabaigh, *Friars*, pp 30–52.

4 Ibid., pp 53–86.

5 Ibid., pp 260–84.

6 Ibid., p. 275. The friary at Drogheda was
also established as a centre for higher
studies.

7 Ibid., p. 274.

8 Gilbert, 'Archives of the town of
Galway', pp 400, 410.

9 Ó Clabaigh, *Friars*, pp 114–15; M.J.
Blake, *Blake family records, 1300–1600*
(London, 1902), pp 17, 25–6, 39.

10 Ó Clabaigh, *Friars*, p. 116.

11 Gilbert, 'Archives of the town of
Galway', p. 396.

12 Gwynn and Hadcock, *Medieval religious
houses*, pp 221, 228, 229. See also Hugh
Fenning, *The Dominicans of Sligo* (Sligo,
2002), pp 7–10.

13 Gwynn and Hadcock, *Medieval religious
houses*, pp 245, 250–1. See also Brendan
Jennings, 'The abbey of St Francis,
Galway', *JGAHS*, 22 (1947), pp 101–19.

14 Gwynn and Hadcock, *Medieval religious
houses*, p. 291; Peter O'Dwyer, *The
Irish Carmelites (of the ancient observance)*
(Dublin, 1988), p. 14. Colmán
Ó Clabaigh, 'The mendicant friars in the
pre-Reformation diocese of Clonfert',
JGAHS, 59 (2007), pp 25–36; F.X.
Martin, 'The Augustinian friaries in
pre-Reformation Ireland', *Augustiniana*,
6 (1956), pp 361–2; Gwynn and
Hadcock, *Medieval religious houses*, p. 296.
For De Clare patronage of monastic
foundations in England, see Karen
Stöber, *Late medieval monasteries and their
patrons: England and Wales, c.1300–1540*
(Cambridge, 2007), pp 162–71.

15 M.J. Blake, 'The obituary book of
the monastery of St Francis, Galway',
JGAHS, 6:4 (1910), pp 222–35 at
pp 227–8.

16 Walsh, 'Account', p. 63.

17 'Brussels MS 3947: *Donatus Moneyus,
De Provincia Hiberniae S. Francisci*', ed.
Brendan Jennings, *Analecta Hibernica*, 6
(1934), pp 12–138 at p. 79. Ó Clabaigh,
Friars, pp 112–17.

18 Hardiman, *History*, pp 241–2.

19 Hardiman, *History*, p. 265. This was later
converted into a sacristy.

20 'Brussels MS 3947', p. 55.

21 Jennings, 'The abbey of St Francis,
Galway', p. 118.

22 O'Flaherty, *Chorographical description*,
pp 418–19.

23 Jennings, 'The abbey of St Francis', p. 118.

24 Hardiman, *History*, p. 266.

25 Ibid., p. 266.

26 *CPR*, xiii, pp 93–4.

27 Blake, 'Old Lynch manuscript', pp 102–3.

28 Thomas Carte, *The life of James, duke
of Ormonde*, 5 vols (Oxford, 1851), ii,
p. 316; v, p. 367.

29 The description was published in
O'Flaherty, *Chorographical description*,
pp 274–5.

30 Indulgences for those venerating the statue on particular Marian feast days were granted to the friars in 1587: Thomas S. Flynn, *The Irish Dominicans, 1536–1641* (Dublin, 1993), pp 87–8.

31 Gwynn and Hadcock, *Medieval religious houses*, p. 300; Martin, 'Augustinian friaries', pp 377–8.

32 Paul Walsh, 'The foundation of the Augustinian friary at Galway: a review of the sources', *JGAHS*, 40 (1985–6), pp 72–80; John O'Connor, *The Galway Augustinians* (Dublin, 1979).

33 William Battersby, *A history of all of the abbeys, convents, churches and other religious houses of the orders, particularly of the hermits of St Augustine in Ireland from the earliest period to the present time* (Dublin, 1856), pp 277–8.

34 Brendan Bradshaw, 'George Browne, first Reformation archbishop of Dublin, 1536–1554', *Journal of Ecclesiastical History*, 21 (1970), pp 301–26.

35 BL, Cotton Augustus MS l.ii, fo. 34; *Cal. Carew MSS*, v, pp 116–17.

36 Battersby, *Hermits of St Augustine*, p. 173.

37 Walsh, *Renaissance Galway*, p. 69.

38 Gwynn and Hadcock, *Medieval religious houses*, p. 289.

39 O'Flaherty, *Chorographical description*, p. 200.

40 Tracy Collins, *Female monasticism in medieval Ireland: an archaeology* (Cork, 2021), p. 66.

41 Mary C. Erler, 'English vowed women at the end of the Middle Ages', *Medieval Studies*, 57 (1995), pp 155–203 at pp 161–3.

42 Ibid., p. 210.

43 Gwynn and Hadcock, *Medieval religious houses*, p. 317.

44 W.W. Seton (ed.), *Two fifteenth-century Franciscan rules* (London, 1914); D.W. Whitfield, 'Third Order of St Francis in medieval England', *Franciscan Studies*, 13 (1953), pp 50–9 at p. 52, suggests it was used by a community of English-speaking tertiaries in Ireland.

45 H. Lemaître, 'Statuts des religieuses du Tiers Ordre Franciscain dites soeurs grises hospitaliers', *Archivium Franciscanum Historicum*, 4 (1911), pp 713–31.

46 Andrea Knox, 'Her booklined cell: Irish nuns and the development of texts, translation and literacy in late medieval Spain' in Virginia Blanton, Veronica O'Mara and Patricia Stoop (eds), *Nuns' literacies in medieval Europe: the Kansas City dialogue* (Turnhout, 2015), pp 67–86 at p. 67.

47 Clyne, 'The founders and patrons', pp 170–1.

48 For the canonical movement in Ireland, see the contributions to Martin Browne and Colmán Ó Clabaigh (eds), *Households of God: the regular canons and canonesses of Saint Augustine and of Prémontré in medieval Ireland* (Dublin, 2019).

49 Jennings, 'Abbey of St Francis', p. 102.

50 Walsh, 'An account', pp 62, 91; Walsh, *Renaissance Galway*, p. 45.

51 Walsh, *Renaissance Galway*, p. 71.

52 McErlean, 'Notes on the pictorial map', p. 151.

53 Helen Nicholson, 'A long way from Jerusalem: the Templars and Hospitallers in Ireland, c.1172–1348' in Browne and Ó Clabaigh (eds), *Soldiers of Christ*, pp 1–22 at p. 9.

5. DEVOTED PEOPLE

1 For a recent treatment of the ritual year in England, see Nicholas Orme, *Going to church in medieval England* (New Haven and London, 2021), pp 197–301. Also, Kevin Danaher, *The year in Ireland* (Cork, 1972).

2 Jim Higgins, 'A fourth Galway Trinity', *JGAHS*, 42 (1990), pp 155–8; Paul Walsh, 'Illustrations of the Holy Trinity in Galway city', *JGAHS*, 43 (1991), pp 173–4. The cathedral ensemble includes an image of the Virgin Mary and a modern carving of the Holy Spirit in the form of a dove.

3 Richard Pfaff, *New liturgical feasts in later medieval England* (Oxford, 1970), pp 62–90.

4 Colmán Ó Clabaigh, 'One bread, one body, one borough: Corpus Christi, Drogheda, 1412' in Brendan Leahy and Salvador Ryan (eds), *Treasures of Irish Christianity: people and place, images and texts* (Dublin, 2012), pp 103–4.

5 Alan Fletcher, 'The civic pageantry of Corpus Christi in fifteenth- and sixteenth-century Dublin', *Irish Economic and Social History*, 23 (1996), pp 73–96.

6 Mary D. O'Sullivan, 'Leisure in Old Galway', *JGAHS*, 18 (1939), pp 99–120 at pp 110–11.

7 Gilbert, 'Archives', p. 387. This latter chapel functioned as a chantry and derived income from various properties in the town. It was administered by its own proctors: see McLysaght and Berry, 'The wardenship of Galway', p. 7.

8 Francesca Sautman, 'Saint Anne in folk tradition: late medieval France' in Kathleen Ashley and Pamela Sheingorn (eds), *Interpreting cultural symbols: Saint Anne in late medieval society* (Athens, GA, and London, 1990), pp 69–95 at p. 81.

9 Myles V. Ronan, *St Anne: her cult and her shrines* (Dublin, 1927), p. 9.

10 Colm Lennon, 'The chantries in the Irish Reformation: the case of St Anne's guild, Dublin' in R.V. Comerford et al. (eds), *Religion, conflict and coexistence in Ireland: essays presented to Monsignor Patrick J. Corish* (Dublin, 1990), pp 6–25, 293–7.

11 Helen M. Roe, 'The cult of St Michael in Ireland' in Caoimhín Ó Danachair, *Folk and farm: essays in honour of A.T. Lucas* (Dublin, 1976), pp 251–64.

12 O'Flaherty, *Chorographical description*, p. 205.

13 Eamon Duffy, *The stripping of the altars* (New Haven and London, 1992), pp 158–9; Edwin Rae, 'The Rice tomb in Waterford Cathedral', *PRIA*, 69C (1970), pp 1–14 at pp 4–8.

14 Bernadette Cunningham, *Medieval Irish pilgrims to Compostela* (Dublin, 2018), pp 114–19, 172, 174. The church/chapel dedications were at Claregalway, Newcastle and Rahoon, while the holy wells were associated with the sites at Rahoon and Newcastle.

15 Ibid., pp 114–18.

16 Colmán Ó Clabaigh, 'The other Christ: the cult of St Francis of Assis in late medieval Ireland' in Rachel Moss, Colmán Ó Clabaigh and Salvador Ryan (eds), *Art and devotion in late medieval Ireland* (Dublin, 2006), pp 142–64.

17 Jim Higgins, pers. comm.

18 Peadar O'Dowd, 'Holy wells of Galway', *JGAHS*, 60 (2008), pp 136–53 at pp 138–45.

19 Ó Clabaigh, *Friars*, pp 187–8.

20 Eamon Duffy, 'Holy maydens, holy wyfes: the cult of women saints in fifteenth- and sixteenth-century England', *Studies in Church History*, 27 (1990), pp 175–96.

21 Theresa O'Byrne, 'Dublin's Hoccleve: James Younge, author and bureaucrat and the literary world of late medieval Dublin' (PhD, Notre Dame, 2012), pp 376–90.

22 Ó Clabaigh, *Friars*, pp 180–8.

23 Gilbert, 'Archives of Galway', p. 391.

24 Ibid., p. 398.

25 Art Cosgrove, 'Marrying and marriage litigation in medieval Ireland' in Philip L. Reynolds and John Witte (eds), *To have and to hold: marrying and its documentation in Western Christendom* (Cambridge, 2009), pp 332–59.

26 Blake, *Blake family records*, p. 17, nos 16, 17; Ó Clabaigh, *Friars*, p. 115.

27 O'Flaherty, *Chorographical description*, pp 216–17.

28 Gilbert, 'Archives of Galway', p. 407.

29 O'Flaherty, *Chorographical description*, pp 198–201.

30 McLysaght and Berry, 'Wardenship of Galway', pp 17–18.

31 O'Flaherty, *Chorographical description*, p. 226; Ó Clabaigh, *Friars*, p. 305.

32 Gilbert, 'Archives of Galway', pp 497, 431.

33 Ibid., p. 387.

34 Ibid., p. 414.

35 Ibid., p. 392.

36 Lennox Barrow, 'Riding the franchises', *Dublin Historical Review*, 33:4 (1980), pp 135–8.

37 McErlean, 'Notes on the pictorial map', pp 148–50; James P. McDonogh, '"Cloch an Loinsigh", Renmore, Galway', *JGAHS*, 34 (1974–5), pp 94–5.

38 For a detailed description of the Rogationtide ritual, see Orme, *Going to church*, pp 288–94.

39 McErlean, 'Notes on the pictorial map', pp 144, 148, 151; Walsh, *Renaissance Galway*, pp 39, 45, 67, 71, 79, 87.

40 For what follows, see Mary D. O'Sullivan, 'Leisure in old Galway', *JGAHS*, 18:3/4 (1939), pp 99–120 at pp 107–13.

41 Gilbert, 'Archives of Galway', pp 398, 410–11.

42 Walsh, *Renaissance Galway*, p. 79.

43 O'Flaherty, *Chorographical description*, p. 60.

44 Gilbert, 'Archives of Galway', p. 414.
45 Danaher, *The year in Ireland*, pp 134–53.
46 Walsh, 'Account', pp 47–118.
47 Hardiman, *History*, p. 53.
48 Walsh, 'Account', p. 61.
49 Walsh, *Renaissance Galway*, p. 67.
50 For a full description and analysis of the building, see David Newnham Johnson, 'Lynch's Castle, Galway city: a reassessment' in Conleth Manning (ed.), *Dublin and beyond the Pale: studies in honour of Paddy Healy* (Dublin, 1998), pp 221–51.
51 The latter quotation is also found on Martin Darcy's house: Walsh, *Renaissance Galway*, p. 55.
52 William Thackery, *Sketches of Ireland* (Dublin, 1842), p. 233 .

53 Coleman, '*Regestum*', p. 210.
54 Ibid., p. 211.
55 Rachel Moss, 'Church plate' in Moss, *Art and architecture of Ireland*, 1, pp 255–9.
56 Raghnall Ó Floinn, 'The Lislaughtin cross' in Griffin Murray (ed.), *Medieval treasures of County Kerry* (Tralee, 2010), pp 82–96.
57 J.J. Buckley, *Some Irish altar plate* (Dublin, 1943), pp 14–18.
58 Blake, 'Old Lynch manuscript', pp 102–3.
59 O'Flaherty, *Chorographical description*, p. 230.
60 Blake, 'Obituary book', p. 224.
61 *Parliamentary Gazetteer* (1844), iv, p. 239.